What are your rights under British 'common law'?

What does sovereignty really mean?

What's a 'rotten borough'?

Operation Chastise was the name for what?

Where did King Cnut come from?

Who invented the game of golf?

What is Sandringham time?

Why should new citizens be friendly with their neighbours?

Can you beat the 51 per cent of British 18–24-year-olds who failed the UK Citizenship test?

The questions in this book are based on the official Home Office handbook, and are like the multiple-choice test that new arrivals need to pass to obtain a British passport.

Filled with obscure questions on British history, culture, government and the law (as well as jaw-dropping statements of the bleeding obvious), chances are that unless you've studied and memorized the book from cover to cover, you'll probably lose the plot.

With Brexit and all this talk of sovereignty, the question of what it really means to be British has never been so important, so here is your chance to see how you measure up to what Your Country Needs You . . . to know.

Grab your family or friends and test yourself – and have a good laugh!

www.penguin.co.uk

The 'Call Yourself British?'
quiz book

Michael Odell

Doubleday

LONDON • TORONTO • SYDNEY • AUCKLAND • JOHANNESBURG

TRANSWORLD PUBLISHERS
61–63 Uxbridge Road, London W5 5SA
www.penguin.co.uk

Transworld is part of the Penguin Random House group of companies
whose addresses can be found at global.penguinrandomhouse.com

First published in Great Britain in 2017 by Doubleday
an imprint of Transworld Publishers

A CIP catalogue record for this book
is available from the British Library.

ISBN 9780857525413

Design and illustrations by Jo Ormiston
Typeset in 11/13pt Times New Roman by Falcon Oast Graphic Art Ltd.
Printed and bound by Clays Ltd, Bungay, Suffolk.

Penguin Random House is committed to a sustainable
future for our business, our readers and our planet. This book
is made from Forest Stewardship Council® certified paper.

3 5 7 9 10 8 6 4

Contents

Introduction

Becoming British has never been more complicated. In the past, the opportunity was open to Huguenot glass-blowers fleeing persecution, Jamaican-born bus drivers, Jewish refugees rescued in the kindertransport or Indians from the Punjab brought over to tackle the Second World War labour shortage. It was even open to a standoffish German family with the surname Saxe-Coburg-Gotha.* As long as you learned to say 'Sorry' every time someone bumped into you in the street, lined up in an orderly queue before aggressively pushing ahead when the bus arrived, and regularly complained about the weather, you could count yourself as British.

But since 2005, an immigrant to this country who wishes to become a British citizen not only has to pass requirements like a speaking and listening test in English, be able to prove they have been continuously resident in the UK for at least five years and be prepared to pay over £1,200 for the privilege, but new arrivals must also pass an official UK citizenship test (cost: an extra £50) to prove they will really fit in.

You count yourself as British, but could YOU pass the test?

It's not as easy as you might think. According to the Home Office, an average of three out of ten applicants for citizenship

---

*The Saxe-Coburg-Gothas changed their name to Windsor in July 1917 so that we would accept them as the British Royal Family.

fail the test. But then, in a 2014 YouGov experiment, a whopping 51 per cent of young people aged 18–24 born and bred in Britain failed to score the required 75 per cent pass level. In a 2013 Ipsos MORI poll for Channel 4, when asked just three taster citizenship questions, only 4 per cent (of a nationally representative sample) got all three right.

In 2012, then prime minister David Cameron told an interviewer that 'Rule, Britannia!' was written by Edward Elgar (it was actually Thomas Arne) and that he had no idea what Magna Carta actually meant (it means 'Great Charter'). You can be sure he wouldn't have passed the test.

Do you know how many members of the Welsh Assembly there are? How many jury members in a Sheriff Court? And do you know what type of animals Stone Age Britons hunted 10,000 years ago? (Note: those bearded bruisers in animal pelt were happily integrated Europeans who had migrated across the land bridge between Britain and the continent of Europe.)

These are all facts laid out in an official book called *Life in the United Kingdom: A Guide for New Residents*. Those who apply for the test are directed to study it in detail. Without doing some serious cramming of the contents, it is unlikely you will pass, no matter how much you think you know about Britain.

The knowledge the Whitehall boffins who devised the test consider you should have in order to become a proper Brit can be surprisingly obscure and arcane. It also reveals a lot about their particular perspective on things. You might be surprised to learn who is the only historical black or Asian immigrant the Home Office has singled out to feature. Have you ever heard of Sake Dean Mahomet? They think you need to know he introduced curry to Britain in 1810. As well as the ancient Indian art of shampooing (head massage). By stark contrast there is not a single mention of Charles Darwin, whose writings did, after all, explain where life on earth came from.

And yet elsewhere, they don't seem to have very high expectations of the level of a candidate's general knowledge or social awareness. For example, the section on pets condescendingly informs: 'A lot of people in the UK have pets such as cats and dogs. They might have them for company or because they enjoy looking after them.' In the section on shopping, they feel it's helpful to explain that: 'There are many different places to go shopping in the UK. Most towns and cities have a central shopping area, which is called the town centre'; and on cooking and food: 'Many people in the UK enjoy cooking. They often invite each other to their homes for dinner. A wide variety of food is eaten in the UK because of the country's rich cultural heritage and diverse population.'

The book manages to offer many other equally bland, patronizing and blindingly obvious explanations: 'Social networking websites such as Facebook and Twitter are a popular way for people to stay in touch with friends, organize social events, and share photos.'

According to a 2009 report, Australians are best at the test – 98 per cent of candidates passed. Nigerians are also pretty good: 82.5 per cent of them were successful. But citizens of the Christmas Islands in the Pacific fared worst, with a 100 per cent failure rate. Having said that, only one person from there has ever attempted it. You will be relieved to know that the Home Office offers a specially adapted citizenship test for Welsh-speaking Patagonians – descendants of the handful of Welsh folk who settled Argentina's desolate southern Chubut Valley in 1865. Although, so far, there has been no demand at all for that test.

But ask yourself: without swotting up on the *Life in the UK* book, how would *you* do in the test? How much do *you* really know about the country in which you live? What does being a

British citizen actually mean? With Brexit a reality, perhaps this is something you now really need to explore.

*

The book is organized in two sections – each with eleven quizzes. The first eleven, UK Citizenship Level, are based on the current Home Office citizenship tests, in that all the information being tested can be found in *Life in the UK*. If you can pass those, you are above averagely knowledgeable about Britain, or a quickly assimilating Johnny Foreigner. On the other hand, scores below 75 per cent mean you not only fail but risk being deported. After that, the only way of gaining re-entry will be either retaking the test or clinging to the underside of a high-speed train through the Channel Tunnel.

The second set of tests, Order of Merit Level, is tougher and the categories of question broader, not just based on the information in the *Life in the UK* book. These are a test of ultimate Britishness. Be warned, the questions will chafe harder than Sir Edmund Hillary's inner thighs on his way up Mount Everest in 1953. Do you know why 'Rule, Britannia!' is, in fact, not a patriotic song, or what is inscribed on the prime minister's letterbox at 10 Downing Street? No? Then don't even *think* about sitting these tests. Go away for a while. Attend Henley Regatta, go and see Millwall play, or compete in the annual cheese-rolling contest at Cooper's Hill in Gloucestershire, then come back and we'll talk again. If you pass these, then you are officially more British than John Bull supping a pint of real ale at a Morris-dancing competition.

Bob's your uncle – and the best of British to you!

QUESTIONS
Section 1: UK Citizenship Level

The following 11 tests are based on the official *Life in the UK* book from the Home Office. At your local official test centre, you would have 45 minutes to sit each test in front of a PC, and you would need to score 75 per cent in order to qualify to become a citizen. So if you haven't got at least 18 out of 24 questions right at the end of every test in Level 1, perhaps you should start packing your bags!

Answers can be found at the back of the book.

> **'The glories of Britain were the plays of Shakespeare, the presumption of innocence, the herbaceous border and the great British breakfast.'**
>
> *John Mortimer*

1. What is the official name of the country in which you live?

A. Great Britain and Northern Ireland

B. The United Kingdom

C. The United Kingdom of Great Britain and Northern Ireland

D. Great Britain

2. Name the service NOT funded by National Insurance Contributions:

A. State retirement pension

B. Civil service pension

C. National Health Service

D. Job Seeker's Allowance

3. TRUE or FALSE: Julius Caesar attempted to invade Britain in 55 BC but was not successful.

4. Where did Britain's first farmers originate?

A. Scotland

B. Wales

C. South-east Europe

D. Devon

> **'Most of [Britain's] inland inhabitants do not sow corn, but live on milk and flesh, and are clad with skins.'**
>
> *Julius Caesar*

5. The British women's suffrage movement gained a major victory in 1918. Who got the vote?

A. All women over 18 with no criminal record who swore allegiance to the Crown

B. All women over 21 with a husband earning more than £10,000 a year

C. All women over 30 who were householders or the wives of householders, occupiers of property with an annual rent of £5, or graduates of British universities

D. All married women who owned at least one acre of UK land with one horse at pasture upon it

6. Which of the following is true?

A. A magistrate is a solicitor with at least 15 years' experience, trained to preside in a court and paid on a judicial stipend

B. A magistrate need have no legal qualifications and works for nothing

C. A magistrate is a retired judge who is paid per sitting

D. A magistrate is a judge who accepts bribes

7. If a person or business owes you £1,000 and refuses to pay, you should:

A. Call the police

B. Call a debt-collection agency

C. Make a small claim online

D. Take them to court

8. What language might you hear spoken in Northern Ireland?

A. Celtic

B. Irish Gaelic

C. Irish Latin

D. Irish English

9. Which of the following is NOT a British invention or discovery?

A. The World Wide Web

B. Cashpoint or ATM

C. DNA

D. Traffic lights

> **'Whatever we invent, from the jet engine to the internet, we find that someone else carts it off and makes a killing from it elsewhere.'**
>
> *Boris Johnson*

10. Which of the following lines is NOT from the national anthem?

A. 'God save your mad parade'

B. 'Frustrate their knavish tricks'

C. 'Scatter her enemies'

D. 'Confound their politics'

11. What is the name of the constitution of the UK?

A. The British Constitution

B. It has no name.

C. The Parliamentary Constitution

D. The Royal Constitution

12. What is another name for the Hindu and Sikh festival Diwali?

A. Festival of Colour

B. Autumn Festival

C. Festival of Deliverance

D. Festival of Lights

13. What did Rudyard Kipling win in 1907?

A. *Great British Bake Off*

B. Victoria Cross

C. The Most Noble Order of the Garter

D. The Nobel Prize in Literature

14. What percentage of the British population has a parent or grandparent born outside the UK?

A. 5 per cent

B. 10 per cent

C. 20 per cent

D. 25 per cent

15. Which of the following is NOT a notable British artist?

A. Thomas Gainsborough

B. David Allan

C. John Masefield

D. John Petts

16. In the UK, all Acts of Parliament are made in the name of:

A. The prime minister

B. God

C. The Queen

D. The Speaker of the House of Commons

17. Since 1958, the prime minister has had the power to:

A. Nominate life peers

B. Sack Members of Parliament who are not doing a good job

C. Spend weekends at Chequers, an official country residence

D. Serve two terms as prime minister

18. TRUE or FALSE: The UK population grew faster between 1901 and 2005 than at any previous time.

19. What TWO things are NOT part of National Citizen Service?

A. Weapons training

B. Taking part in a community project

C. A citizenship test

D. Litter picking

20. What preceded the Iron Age in Britain?

A. The Stone Age

B. The Neolithic Age

C. The Brass Age

D. The Bronze Age

> **'The Muppet Show is pretty much exactly the present state of British politics.'**
>
> *Caitlin Moran*

21. What happened as a result of the Acts of Union in 1800?

A. Ireland united with England, Wales and Scotland to form the United Kingdom

B. England and France signed a peace treaty

C. Northern Ireland united with southern Ireland

D. Scotland united with England

22. When a woman got married in the 1960s, it was not unusual for:

A. An employer to ask her to leave her job

B. Her husband to demand she get a job

C. An employer to cut her pay

D. An employer to offer maternity pay and childcare vouchers

23. Name TWO major achievements of the architect Sir Edwin Lutyens:

A. He designed the Cenotaph war memorial in Whitehall

B. He designed Princess Victoria's dolls' house

C. He designed New Delhi as the British Indian Empire's seat of government

D. He designed the white cliffs of Dover and organized the dynamiting which created them

24. TRUE or FALSE: You must be certified dead before you can donate a kidney in the UK

Find the answers to this test on p.186.

'We are a small country with a
large sense of its own importance.'

David Walliams

T
E
S
T

2

1. What or who is Skara Brae?

A. A type of goat

B. A prehistoric king

C. A type of cheese

D. A prehistoric village

2. Why was landscape designer Lancelot 'Capability' Brown so called?

A. Because King George III said he could transform 'a slurry pit into an Eden'

B. Because he showed the possibilities of using the first mechanical diggers

C. Because he sired 14 children during his lifetime, nine of whom became gardeners

D. Because he often said a place 'had capabilities'

3. Which country left the Commonwealth in 2013?

A. Swaziland

B. The Gambia

C. Maldives

D. Lesotho

4. What was the purpose of the 1833 Emancipation Act?

A. Women to have the right to vote

B. Slaves to be freed and slavery made illegal

C. Factory workers to be paid a minimum wage

D. Wives to have the right to divorce their husbands for the first time

'That's definitely the trouble with upper-class Englishmen – they just can't drive past a perversion without pulling over.'

Kathy Lette

5. Who won an Olympic gold medal for Britain in the pentathlon in 1972?

A. Henry Cooper

B. Alan Minter

C. Mary Peters

D. Jane Torville

6. What does the Council of Europe do?

A. Agrees trade between European countries

B. Passes European laws

C. Upholds human rights among EU member states

D. Resolves disagreements between member states

7. When was the voting age reduced to 18 for men and women?

A. 1918

B. 1928

C. 1956

D. 1969

8. The Man Booker Prize for Fiction is open to submissions from:

A. A male novelist from anywhere in the world

B. A male novelist from the Commonwealth, Ireland or Zimbabwe

C. A novelist of any gender from the Commonwealth, Ireland or Zimbabwe

D. A novelist who has never been published before

> **'The average Englishman goes six months without crying, depending on football results.'**
>
> *Frank Skinner*

9. TRUE or FALSE: During the Middle Ages, England was closed to foreign migrants.

10. What is English 'common law'?

A. The law applied to working-class people

B. The law applied according to precedence and tradition

C. The law applied to co-habiting but unmarried partners

D. The law applied to grazing rights on common ground

11. TRUE or FALSE: Women won the right to divorce their husbands in 1800.

12. Who was known as the Iron Duke?

A. Napoleon

B. The Duke of Wellington

C. Denis Thatcher (husband of Mrs Thatcher, aka the Iron Lady)

D. The Duke of Earl

13. Which poem is this line from: 'What passing-bells for these who die as cattle?'

A. 'In Flanders Fields' by John McCrae

B. 'Anthem for Doomed Youth' by Wilfred Owen

C. 'As Flies to Wanton Boys' by Pam Ayres

D. 'The Soldier' by Rupert Brooke

14. A Forced Marriage Protection Order can do which TWO of the following:

A. Protect a person from being forced into a marriage

B. Protect a person already in a forced marriage

C. Ensure a forced marriage is declared void

D. Ensure a forced marriage runs as smoothly as possible

15. What language did Iron Age Britons speak?

A. English

B. Celtic

C. Roman

D. Ironic

16. What is the distance from John o' Groats in Scotland to Land's End in Cornwall?

A. 550 miles

B. 760 miles

C. 820 miles

D. 870 miles

17. Which of the following is an important part of the UK character according to *Life in the UK*?

A. To keep a stiff upper lip

B. To root for the underdog

C. To be watchful of foreigners in our country

D. The ability to laugh at ourselves

18. TRUE or FALSE: The House of Commons has the power to overrule the House of Lords.

19. What is the name of the system by which MPs are elected?

A. Cash for questions

B. Proportional representation

C. Tactical voting

D. First past the post

20. Where did TV comedians Morecambe and Wise begin their career?

A. Music halls

B. Cruise ships

C. Performing for the troops during the Second World War

D. *That Was the Week That Was*

'We always have been, we are, and I hope that we always shall be, detested in France.'

Duke of Wellington

21. What is another name for the Union Jack flag?

A. The Union flag

B. The Jolly Roger

C. The St George flag

D. The tricolour flag

22. Who is the author of *The Jungle Book*?

A. Mowgli

B. Walt Disney

C. Rudyard Kipling

D. Beatrix Potter

23. What was the so-called 'Butler Act' of 1944 about?

A. New employment legislation for all domestic staff

B. Free education for all domestic staff

C. Free secondary education for all children in England and Wales

D. Introduction of grammar schools in England

24. A new British citizen must swear an oath of allegiance to the monarch and who else?

A. The prime minister

B. The Archbishop of Canterbury

C. The monarch's heirs and successors

D. The chief constable of England and Wales

'Education isn't everything.
For a start, it's not elephants.'

Spike Milligan

Find the answers to this test on p.190.

T
E
S
T

2

> **'I shall tell you what is so good
> about England: it is the only country
> in the world that isn't semi-detached.'**
>
> *Captain Peacock,* Are You Being Served?

**T
E
S
T**

3

1. The Magna Carta was signed by King John in 1215. What did it secure?

A. A large cart for every free yeoman to put before a horse

B. The King's right to collect taxes

C. The right to justice for every man regardless of social status

D. The right for every man to own land

2. Members of the Welsh Assembly are known as:

A. MPs (Members of Parliament)

B. WMPs (Welsh Members of Parliament)

C. MWPs (Members of Welsh Parliament)

D. AMs (Assembly Members)

3. Which of these countries is NOT a member of the EU?

A. Albania

B. Slovakia

C. Slovenia

D. United Kingdom

4. Which of these countries is part of Great Britain?

A. St Helena

B. The Isle of Man

C. Northern Ireland

D. Scotland

5. James II of England was known by a different title in Scotland. Was it:

A. James VI

B. James III

C. James VII

D. William II

'This once glorious land of Henry the Eighth and West Ham United.'

Alf Garnett, Till Death Us Do Part

6. On which of the following is income tax not payable?

A. If paid in cash

B. If you're self-employed

C. If you are a pensioner

D. A gift

7. Which country of the United Kingdom does not have its symbol included in the Union Jack?

A. England

B. Scotland

C. Wales

D. Northern Ireland

8. What features of cricket are said to reflect the best of the British character?

A. The fact that one player is called 'silly mid-on'

B. The players wear 'whites', which easily attract grass stains

C. Games can last for five days and still end in a draw

D. Tea is served during the interval

9. Who was Kenneth MacAlpin and why is he important?

A. He was a pioneering builder who founded a major construction company

B. He was a Scottish barrister and pioneer of Scottish independence

C. He was the geologist who discovered Scotland's vast oil reserves

D. He was the king who united Scotland against the Viking

10. Sir Arthur Conan Doyle invented Sherlock Holmes, one of the first fictional detectives. What was his other occupation?

A. He was an engineer who invented the first tank

B. He was a ship's surgeon on a whaling ship

C. He was a Scottish priest

D. He was a chess grandmaster

11. What were Bronze Age people buried in?

A. Pits

B. Stone circles

C. Barrows

D. Mounds

12. The White Tower in the Tower of London is an example of:

A. The usual casual racist bias

B. A Norman grain store

C. An early effort to build a structure to house and protect the resident ravens

D. A Norman castle keep

> '[When the BBC first broadcast to the USA], it took a team of translators a week to figure out that "bangers and mash" were not some veiled British threat.'
>
> *President Bill Clinton*

13. Name TWO ways the Suffragettes campaigned for women's voting rights:

A. They held cake sales

B. They broke windows and committed arson

C. They went on hunger strike

D. They kidnapped leading politicians

14. A million soldiers from which country fought alongside Britain in the First World War?

A. New Zealand

B. Australia

C. India

D. Canada

15. What date is St George's Day?

A. 23 April

B. 3 April

C. 1 May

D. 21 June

16. What percentage of the UK identifies as Christian?

A. 71 per cent

B. 43 per cent

C. 28 per cent

D. 59 per cent

17. How often is a General Election held?

A. At least every four years

B. At least every five years

C. At least every two years

D. Whenever the prime minister wants to call one

> **'Most Englishmen, if forced into analysing their own creeds – which heaven forbid – are convinced that God is an Englishman, probably educated at Eton.'**
>
> *E. M. Delafield*

18. What is the Church of England called in Scotland?

A. The Sassenach Church

B. The Episcopal Church

C. The Anglican Church

D. The Reformation Church

19. What does 'the Pale' refer to in Irish history?

A. A derogatory word for English invaders

B. An area around Dublin ruled by the English in the Middle Ages

C. A bucket filled with faeces thrown over English invaders

D. A fortified fence around the castle of the Irish king

20. Which group of immigrants came to Britain between 1870 and 1914 to escape persecution and settled in London's East End, Manchester and Leeds?

A. Pakistanis

B. South Africans

C. Russian and Polish Jews

D. Irish

21. Who raised the rallying cry 'No taxation without representation'?

A. Factory workers during the Industrial Revolution

B. Voters in rotten boroughs

C. Citizens in British colonies of North America

D. Female factory workers who did not have the vote

22. Why did Henry VIII establish the Church of England?

A. To appoint his own bishops

B. The Pope would not give permission for his divorce

C. His second bride wanted to marry in an English church with English liturgy

D. He didn't think the Pope was doing a good enough job

23. Where is a 16-year-old allowed to drink beer or wine?

A. In their own home when supervised by an adult

B. In a hotel or restaurant when eating with someone aged 18 or over

C. In a pub garden or family room

D. Wherever their parents drink

> **'I love the pageantry of England. The Queen can't help what she was born into. She's a dear old thing and I'll miss her when she's gone.'**
>
> *John Lydon, aka Johnny Rotten*

24. What was the name of the government of the English republic after the execution of Charles I in 1649?

A. The Commonwealth

B. The Commons

C. The Roundhead Parliament

D. The Protectorate

Find the answers to this test on p.195.

Section 1: Test 4

**'The only possible way
there'd be an uprising in
this country is if they banned
car boot sales and
caravanning.'**

Victoria Wood

1. What is the Children's Hearings System?

A. The NHS department for young people who are deaf
   or hard of hearing

B. The Scottish court for young offenders

C. The hearings that precede the Youth Court in England

D. A Roman court for young offenders

2. Who decides the hours that a pub or nightclub is open?

A. The local council

B. The police

C. The bar staff

D. The licensee

3. Prior to the Reform Acts of the nineteenth century, parliamentary constituencies controlled by a single wealthy person or family were known as:

A. Rackman boroughs

B. Pocket boroughs

C. Family seats

D. Squiredoms

4. What did James Goodfellow invent in the 1960s?

A. The X-ray machine

B. The skateboard

C. The ATM (or cashpoint)

D. The pill

5. Who was responsible for the foundation of the Paralympic Games?

A. A German refugee living in Buckinghamshire

B. A paraplegic refugee insurance clerk

C. A partially sighted Polish high-jumper

D. A one-armed Italian shot-putter

6. Which of these organizations does not work as a parliamentary lobby group?

A. The Confederation of British Industry (CBI)

B. Greenpeace

C. Ofcom

D. Liberty

7. TRUE or FALSE: The devolved administrations in Wales, Scotland and Northern Ireland are served by the English civil service in Whitehall.

8. Richard Arkwright was a barber who eventually became famous for:

A. The mass production of wigs

B. Creating the first modern hairstyles

C. Pioneering steam-powered textile machinery

D. Building the first London to Leeds railway

9. Which of the following is a place Winston Churchill said the British would fight the Germans?

A. The hills

B. The alleyways

C. The shores

D. The roads

10. What caused 1.5 million Irish to abandon their country in the nineteenth century?

A. Superior job prospects in America's construction industry

B. The Irish flu

C. A widespread famine

D. Violence between Republicans and Loyalists

'Oh the things I do for England!'

James Bond

11. Which of the following is NOT a stated responsibility of a British citizen?

A. To vote in local and national government elections

B. To help and protect your family

C. To behave responsibly

D. To protect and fight for your country

12. How were the Wars of the Roses resolved?

A. With the Treaty of London

B. A negotiated settlement between Henry Tudor and Richard III

C. Parliament declared Henry Tudor king

D. With a battle at Bosworth Field

13. Where was British Olympic champion Mo Farah born?

A. South Sudan

B. Manchester

C. Senegal

D. Somalia

14. TRUE or FALSE: The Scottish and Welsh parliaments can make their own civil and criminal law.

15. The style in which the Houses of Parliament and London's St Pancras station are both built is known as:

A. Grandiose Romantic

B. Neoclassical

C. Gothic Revival

D. Victorian Baroque

'The one great principle of English law is to make business for itself.'

Charles Dickens

16. Why did the Roman army leave Britain in AD 410?

A. To defend the Roman Empire under attack elsewhere

B. Having brought Britain straight roads, plumbing and bureaucracy, they felt they were no longer needed

C. The Emperor Claudius decreed the cost of maintaining an army in Britain 'unaffordable'

D. Romans were unable to defeat the Jutes, the Angles and the Saxons

17. Which ONE thing did the 1689 Bill of Rights NOT demand?

A. The monarch must be born British

B. The monarch must be a Protestant

C. A new Parliament must be elected every three years

D. The monarch must request funding for the army and navy every year

18. Who took the title Lord Protector in the 1640s?

A. King Charles I

B. Oliver Cromwell

C. King Charles II

D. Richard the Lionheart

19. TRUE or FALSE: The Northern Ireland Parliament was established in 1922.

20. Who is allowed access to the electoral register?

A. The mayor

B. The chief of the electoral roll and the mayor

C. Businesses which have a special relationship with the local council

D. Everyone

> **'It's not the voting that is democracy, it's the counting.'**
>
> *Tom Stoppard*

21. Charles Dickens' character Mr Micawber is noted for what quality?

A. He is always optimistic

B. He is always hungry

C. He doesn't suffer fools gladly

D. He is thrifty

22. TRUE or FALSE: The Angles and Saxons conquered the whole of Britain.

23. What happened to the English language between 1066 and 1400?

A. It was superseded by Norman French

B. It absorbed some Norman French influences and became the official language

C. It was spoken by peasants but Norman French became the language of government

D. It co-existed with Norman French and Celtic

24. In Wales, what is the Senedd?

A. The ruling body of the Welsh church

B. The Welsh Assembly building

C. The site where St David was eaten by a dragon

D. The home of Welsh rugby's ruling body, the WRU

'You can get any Englishman to do anything you want simply by whispering in his ear: "I know your guilty secret."'

P. G. Wodehouse

Find the answers to this test on p.199.

'Your question for £10:
What is the capital of
England? Is it:
a) London
b) Somewhere else
c) Somewhere else entirely
d) A worm.'

French and Saunders

1. What does the Bayeux Tapestry commemorate?

A. The Grand Bayeux embroidery competition of 1267

B. The Anglo-Saxon defeat of the Vikings

C. The Norman Conquest of 1066

D. Charlemagne's victory over the Saxons in 782

2. The Black Death of 1348 killed one third of the population of England, Scotland and Wales. Which of the following was NOT a result of this plague?

A. Reduced demand for cereal crops

B. Peasants demanded higher wages

C. Public sewers were introduced in London

D. New social classes including 'the gentry' and 'the middle class' were formed

3. How many houses did the early Scottish parliament have?

A. Three: Lords, Commons and Clergy

B. Two: Lords and Commons

C. One: Commons

D. Four: Scots Chamber, English Chamber, Lords, Commons

4. The Battle of Trafalgar was fought between:

A. Britain and France

B. Britain against France and Spain

C. Britain against France and the Netherlands

D. Britain and Spain against the French

5. Who wrote the line 'Oh to be in England now that April's there'?

A. William Wordsworth

B. John Keats

C. Robert Browning

D. Nigel Farage

'If you lead a country like Britain, a strong country, a country which has taken a lead in world affairs in good times and in bad, a country that is always reliable, then you have to have a touch of iron about you.'

Margaret Thatcher

6. Who discovered insulin as a treatment for diabetes?

A. Sir Tim Berners-Lee

B. Sir Robert Watson-Watt

C. Sir Peter Mansfield

D. John Macleod

7. Who directed the 1949 film *The Third Man*?

A. Sir Richard Attenborough

B. Sir Ridley Scott

C. Sir Carol Reed

D. Sir David Lean

8. Which TWO are NOT core values of the Commonwealth?

A. Good government

B. Rule of law

C. Allegiance to the Crown

D. Pride in British culture

9. Which of the following are TWO areas of civil law (as opposed to criminal law)?

A. Shoddy work by a builder

B. Being drunk on an aircraft

C. Excessive bank charges

D. Smoking in a public place

10. How would Britons have travelled to mainland Europe 10,000 years ago?

A. They never did

B. On foot

C. By raft and early boats

D. By swimming, occasionally catching a lift on a porpoise

11. A single TV licence is enough for one house except when:

A. There is more than one TV

B. Any one viewer is a top-rate taxpayer

C. A person is renting a room and has a separate tenancy agreement

D. They are employees of the BBC

> ### 'The House of Lords is the British Outer Mongolia for retired politicians.'
> *Tony Benn*

12. Since 1999, hereditary peers have lost the right to:

A. Automatically inherit a title

B. Automatically attend the House of Lords

C. Fall asleep while House of Lords business is being conducted

D. Vote in elections

13. What is Scottish poet Robert Burns's most famous work?

A. 'Scotland the Brave'

B. 'Auld Lang Syne'

C. *Ballamory*

D. 'Mull of Kintyre'

14. During the Industrial Revolution, the Bessemer process was a way of mass producing:

A. Steel

B. Bread

C. Cotton

D. Beer

15. Who established the NHS in 1948?

A. William Beveridge

B. Bev Bevan

C. Clement Attlee

D. Aneurin Bevan

16. What was the Danelaw?

A. The Viking legal code

B. The area of Britain settled by Vikings

C. The first example of British food standards, applied to Danish bacon

D. The oath taken by Viking warriors prior to battle

17. When did *all* UK women win the right to vote at the same age as men?

A. 1928

B. 1945

C. 1973

D. 1978

18. How many candles are there on a menorah during Hanukkah?

A. Six

B. Seven

C. Eight

D. Nine

19. For some Scots, what occasion is bigger than Christmas?

A. Easter

B. New Year

C. World Cup finals

D. St Andrew's Day

> 'A family with the wrong members in control; that, perhaps, is as near as one can come to describing England in a phrase.'
>
> *George Orwell*

20. How old must you be to stand for election to Parliament?

A. 18

B. 21

C. 25

D. 30

21. Which sport did NOT originate in Britain?

A. Golf

B. Tennis

C. Football

D. Polo

'I do love cricket – it's so very English.'

Sarah Bernhardt,
on watching a game of football

22. Who founded the National Trust in 1895?

A. Queen Victoria's gamekeeper and Master of the Royal Parks

B. Three anonymous volunteers

C. Three members of the House of Lords

D. Joseph Paxton

23. What happens at the National Eisteddfod of Wales?

A. Welsh chefs compete to create the best Welsh dish

B. Welsh music, dance and poetry is performed

C. Members of the Welsh rugby team are chosen

D. Welsh choirs compete for the national championship cup

24. Where does the Scottish Grand National take place?

A. Aintree – it immediately follows the English one

B. There isn't one – the Grand National at Aintree covers the whole of the UK

C. Ayr

D. Hamilton Park

Find the answers to this test on p.203.

Find the answers to this test on p.203.

Section 1: Test 6

Q

'You cannot trust people
who have such bad cuisine.
It is the country with the
worst food after Finland.'

French president *Jacques Chirac*

1. What is the largest expanse of fresh water in Britain?

A. Ullswater, Lake District

B. Windermere, Lake District

C. Loch Lomond

D. Rutland Water

2. What did scientists Sir Ian Wilmut and Keith Campbell succeed in doing in 1996?

A. They created the first test-tube baby

B. They created the World Wide Web

C. They cloned a sheep

D. They were behind the world's first face transplant

3. Iron Age Britons were the first to introduce what to Britain?

A. Metal spear tips

B. The wheel

C. Coins

D. An iron

4. What did the Chartists campaign for?

A. The accurate representation of Britain as further away from Europe on all maps and charts

B. Voting rights for the working class

C. The abolition of the death penalty for cases other than treason or murder

D. The abolition of the monarchy and the establishment of a republic like that of France

5. Henry VIII's wife Anne Boleyn was unpopular because:

A. She was accused of poisoning her predecessor, Catherine of Aragon

B. She was accused of adultery

C. She was accused of taking bribes

D. She was blamed for the King's obesity

6. What ONE ingredient is NOT found in Scottish haggis?

A. Sheep's stomach

B. Onions

C. Oats

D. Carrots

7. The European Economic Community was formed in 1957. When did the UK join?

A. 1964

B. 1971

C. 1973

D. 1990

8. What did writer Roald Dahl do before he became known as a writer?

A. He served in the RAF

B. He was a British Army officer

C. He was a government minister

D. He was a director of Cadbury's

> **'The English people fancy they are free; it is only during the election of Members of Parliament that they are so. As soon as these are elected the people are slaves.'**
>
> *Jean-Jacques Rousseau*

9. TRUE or FALSE: Anyone on the electoral register can be selected to serve on a jury.

10. Who was Boudicca?

A. The first Roman queen in Britain

B. Queen of the Iceni tribe who fought the Romans

C. Queen of the Angles who fought the Saxons

D. Queen of the Saxons who fought the Normans

> ## 'I would rather be a rebel than a slave.'
> *Emmeline Pankhurst*

11. What production has enjoyed the longest initial run in theatre history?

A. *Hamlet* by William Shakespeare

B. *The Mousetrap* by Agatha Christie

C. *The Rat Trap* by Noël Coward

D. *Phantom of the Opera* by Andrew Lloyd Webber

12. Members of the Northern Ireland Assembly are known as:

A. MPs

B. MAs

C. MLAs

D. NAMs

13. Give TWO habits *Life in the UK* says may cause conflict with your neighbour:

A. Putting out refuse bags in communal areas or on the street when it's not bin day

B. Putting out champagne bottles in your recycling and other conspicuous displays of consumption

C. Allowing your garden to become untidy

D. Having an affair with a member of the neighbouring family

14. Which ONE is NOT a constitutional institution in the UK?

A. The police

B. The cabinet

C. The judiciary

D. *The Archers*

15. What does the Vaisakhi festival mark?

A. The cessation of hostilities between Britain and Japan in the Second World War

B. The founding of the Sikh order

C. The founding of the Hindu community

D. The victory of the Maori people over Fijian invaders

16. Why did Roman Emperor Hadrian build a wall?

A. To keep the Picts out

B. To keep the Britons in

C. To keep the Scots out

D. To keep Mexicans out

17. What was another name for the 1942 Social Insurance and Allied Services report?

A. The NHS Report

B. The Beveridge Report

C. The Welfare State Report

D. The UK Social Security Report

'I can speak English, I learn it from a book'

Manuel, Fawlty Towers

18. What did Sir Francis Drake achieve in his ship the *Golden Hind*?

A. He was the first Englishman to circumnavigate the globe

B. He was the first sailor to bring a cargo of tobacco to England

C. He was the first Englishman to navigate by compass and sextant

D. He was the first sailor to reach America

19. In 1847, British law prohibited children from working in factories:

A. At any time

B. More than four hours a day

C. More than ten hours a day

D. If they had a criminal record

20. Who appoints the government in Britain?

A. The electorate

B. The monarch

C. The prime minister

D. The media

21. Where are minor criminal cases dealt with in Scotland?

A. A Justice of the Peace Court

B. A Magistrates' Court

C. A Hogmanay Court

D. A Sheriff Court

22. Drivers can use their driving licence until they are 70. After that:

A. They are banned from driving

B. They may only drive a car capable of 50mph or less

C. They are banned from driving at night

D. Their licence is only renewed for three years at a time

23. Which British composer wrote the music for the hymn 'I Vow To Thee My Country'?

A. Sir Edward Elgar

B. Ralph Vaughan Williams

C. Gustav Holst

D. George Frederick Handel

24. In 1560, the Parliament of Scotland refused to recognize the Pope. What happened as a result?

A. Scottish Catholics moved to England

B. Roman Catholic religious services were banned in Scotland

C. The Pope excommunicated the Scots

D. Mary, Queen of Scots, a Catholic, returned to Scotland from France

Find the answers to this test on p.207.

T
E
S
T
6

Section 1: Test 7

Q

'A traditional fixture at
Wimbledon is the way the
BBC TV commentary box fills
up with British players
eliminated in the early rounds.'

Clive James

1. Which TWO nations have a public holiday on their national saint's day?

A. England

B. Scotland

C. Northern Ireland

D. Wales

2. Name TWO things Protestants did differently from Catholics in the sixteenth century:

A. They didn't read the Bible in Latin

B. They did not kneel while praying

C. They did not pray to saints

D. They did not eat fish on Friday

3. Who wrote 'Music for the Royal Fireworks'?

A. Elton John

B. George Frederick Handel

C. Henry Purcell

D. Guy Fawkes

4. Who or what is Vindolanda?

A. A fifteenth-century pre-Colombian map of America

B. A Roman fort

C. A Roman warrior

D. A Roman window company

5. TRUE or FALSE: The Easter Rising of 1916 successfully drove the British out of Ireland and it became a Republic.

6. During the Great Depression in the 1930s, what happened to British car ownership?

A. It decreased from one million to half a million

B. It doubled from one to two million

C. It stayed at roughly one million

D. By 1934, there were only 500 cars left in Britain

Q

7. What did Sir Roger Bannister achieve in 1954?

A. He invented the stairlift

B. He ran a mile in under four minutes

C. He ran 100 yards in under ten seconds

D. He ran the marathon in under four hours

8. In what order did Henry VIII marry his wives?

A. Catherine of Aragon, Anne Boleyn, Jane Seymour, Anne of Cleves, Catherine Howard, Catherine Parr

B. Jane Seymour, Anne Boleyn, Catherine of Aragon, Anne of Cleves, Catherine Parr, Catherine Howard

C. Anne Boleyn, Catherine Howard, Jane Seymour, Catherine of Aragon, Catherine Parr, Anne of Cleves

D. Catherine Parr, Anne of Cleves, Catherine of Aragon, Jane Seymour, Anne Boleyn, Catherine Howard

9. The 1832 Reform Act established more parliamentary seats for:

A. Pocket boroughs

B. Towns and cities

C. The working class

D. Rural districts

'I fall in love with Britain every day, with bridges, buses, blue skies . . . but it's a brutal world, man.'

Pete Doherty

10. What is Jodrell Bank?

A. The Royal Mint's bullion store

B. Apart from Coutts, it is the only British bank catering exclusively to millionaires

C. A radio telescope

D. The main listening station for GCHQ

11. What did Alexander Fleming discover in 1928?

A. The flu virus

B. A cure for malaria

C. A cure for tuberculosis

D. Penicillin

12. Who was elected prime minister after the war in 1945?

A. Winston Churchill

B. Clement Attlee

C. Aneurin Bevin

D. Harold Macmillan

'There are hardly two things more peculiarly English than Welsh rarebit and Irish stew.'

G. K. Chesterton

13. Under UK law, in a married couple, who is most responsible for childcare?

A. The mother, if she is not working full-time

B. The mother – end of

C. The father, as long as the child is not presenting 'unusual emotional need'

D. Both are equally responsible.

14. In the 2011 Census, what percentage of people in the UK said they had no religion?

A. 12 per cent

B. 18 per cent

C. 25 per cent

D. 52 per cent

15. Who selects the Archbishop of Canterbury?

A. The House of Lords

B. The Queen, acting through the prime minister

C. The prime minister, acting through the Queen

D. The UK Council of Robes and Prelates

16. Why did the English Civil War erupt in 1642?

A. Parliament wouldn't give Charles I money to fight the Scots and Irish

B. Charles I wouldn't give Parliament money for a new roof

C. Parliament refused to give Charles I money for his coronation

D. Charles I and Parliament couldn't agree on who to attack first, Scotland or Ireland

> **'Britain is like Mini-Me to America's Dr Evil – helping out in all our zany schemes to take over the world.'**
>
> *Marge Simpson*

17. What were British bus company executives doing in the West Indies in the 1950s?

A. Building a bus factory with cheap local labour

B. Teaching locals how to establish a local bus service

C. Sourcing spare parts

D. Recruiting workers to emigrate to the UK to drive buses

18. Why was the term the Swinging Sixties originally coined?

A. Execution by hanging reached a peak

B. To mark a time of sexual and social liberation and the emergence of a distinct British pop music and fashion culture

C. It was a time of extreme political swings from right to left

D. Couples sharing partners, or 'swinging', became popular and was much written about in the tabloid press

19. After the Romans left Britain, who invaded next?

A. The Normans

B. The Spanish

C. Angles and Saxons

D. The Celts

'Sodding, blimey, shaggin', knickers, bollocks. Oh, God, I'm turning English.'

Spike, Buffy the Vampire Slayer

20. Name TWO ways to visit the Northern Ireland Assembly at Stormont:

A. By booking a ticket through visitor services or through www.irishlandmark.com

B. By just turning up – entrance is free and open to all

C. By contacting the Education Service

D. By contacting an MLA (Member of the Legislative Assembly)

21. Of how many countries is Queen Elizabeth II monarch?

A. One

B. Four

C. 16

D. 154

22. What happens at the Cornish Eden Project?

A. The Garden of Eden has been re-created using the latest biblical research

B. Plant life from around the world is showcased

C. Cornish life and culture through the ages is celebrated

D. Animal and plant life from around the world is showcased

23. In the UK electoral system, what is the name for the collective number of people who can vote ?

A. The electorate

B. The constituency

C. The franchise

D. The ballot

24. What is the main reason the UK does not have a written constitution?

A. It did, but the document was burned during the Civil War

B. The population was largely illiterate until the 1600s, so the tradition is to pass it down orally

C. Unlike France or America, revolutionary movements in the UK have never led to a permanent and complete change in the system of government

D. Because the Scots, Welsh and Irish would not agree on terms or for it to be written in English

Find the answers to this quiz on p.212.

> ## 'I left England when I was four because I found out I could never be king.'
>
> *Bob Hope*

1. The Divine Right of Kings encapsulated the idea that:

A. The monarch and his retinue can drive on the right, though everyone else must drive on the left

B. The monarch is appointed by God and can rule without consulting Parliament

C. The monarch is appointed by God, but Parliament rules supreme

D. The monarch's rights are limited, but he or she retains the right to declare war on other nations

2. The automatic collection of taxes from employee income is known as:

A. Pay All You Earn

B. National Insurance

C. Pay As You Earn

D. Pay After You Earn

3. Who was the first Briton to sail single-handed non-stop around the world?

A. Sir Francis Drake

B. Sir Francis Chichester

C. Bear Grylls

D. Sir Robin Knox-Johnston

> **'Any damn fool can navigate the world sober. It takes a really good sailor to do it drunk.'**
>
> *Sir Francis Chichester*

4. Where is the National Horseracing Museum?

A. Ascot

B. Nagton

C. Newmarket

D. Lingfield

5. What TWO skills did French Huguenots bring to Britain when they came fleeing persecution?

A. Banking

B. Weaving

C. Cheese-making

D. Wine-making

> '**One of the things I most love about this country is that we do not, will not, stare at each other . . . In a cramped, crowded nation, we know the essence of politeness is ignoring pretty much everyone around us.**'
>
> *Caitlin Moran*

6. Acts of Parliament in 1870 and 1882 gave married women:

A. The vote

B. The right to retain their own earnings and property

C. The right to a fair trial

D. The right to half their husband's wealth in divorce

7. Which ONE of the following was NOT a demand of the Chartists in the 1830s and '40s?

A. Elections to be held every year

B. MPs to be paid a salary

C. Secret ballots

D. Subsidized MPs' bar in the House of Commons

8. Where did King Cnut come from?

A. Norway

B. Denmark

C. England

D. Scotland

9. Which of the following is a renowned painter of royal portraits who died in 1941?

A. James McNeill Whistler

B. Sir Joshua Banksy

C. Rolf Harris

D. Sir John Lavery

10. London's Tate Modern used to be:

A. A power station

B. A recycling centre

C. A prison

D. A shipping warehouse

11. Which TWO animals did early Britons hunt?

A. Mammoth

B. Wild boar

C. Deer

D. Horses

12. Which of the following was NOT drafted by the British?

A. The Magna Carta

B. The European Convention on Human Rights

C. The Bill of Rights, 1791

D. The Bill of Rights, 1689

13. Why do the British eat pancakes on Shrove Tuesday?

A. The pancake symbolizes our sins, for which we will atone and pay penance during Lent

B. To use up eggs, fat and milk before fasting during Lent

C. Tossing the pancake symbolizes the 'feast before fast', before Lent

D. The lemon squeezed on pancakes symbolizes the sour experience of Jesus' fast

> 'He that but looketh on a plate of ham and eggs to lust after it, hath already committed breakfast with it in his heart.'
>
> C. S. Lewis

14. The British Empire in the Victorian Age was:

A. Almost as large as the French empire

B. Almost as large as the Roman Empire

C. The largest empire the world has ever seen

D. In decline after the loss of the American colonies

15. Name the famous radio play by Dylan Thomas:

A. *Dairy Milk Wood*

B. *Under Milk Wood*

C. *The War of the Worlds*

D. *Portrait of the Artist as a Young Cow*

16. The post-war 'welfare state' promised a system of benefits to protect people:

A. 'In all times of strain, want or hardship'

B. 'When the ugly spectre of hunger or privation looms'

C. 'From cradle to the grave'

D. 'When the alms of family and community fail'

17. What did Charles II do after the Battle of Worcester?

A. He became king of Scotland

B. He became king of England

C. He hid in a chestnut tree

D. He hid in an oak tree

18. Forced marriage, where full consent is not given by both parties, is:

A. Another name for arranged marriage

B. A criminal offence

C. Legal only if you are related

D. Also referred to as a 'shotgun marriage'

19. TRUE or FALSE: A Liechtenstein driving licence is valid in the UK.

> ### 'The English never know
> ### when they are beaten.'
> Spanish saying

**T
E
S
T**

8

20. What caused a serious famine in Ireland in the nineteenth century?

A. Civil war wrecked the country's agriculture

B. The British navy blockaded food imports

C. The potato crop failed

D. The Irish pound collapsed

21. What power does the monarch have over the prime minister?

A. The power to dissolve Parliament

B. The power to advise, warn and encourage

C. The power to sack

D. The power to overrule

22. In which sport is the Super League the main club competition?

A. Stock car racing

B. Point-to-point horse racing

C. Rugby league

D. Football

23. What was known as the 'Glorious Revolution'?

A. The restoration of Charles II as king

B. The overthrow of King James II and accession of William and Mary without violence

C. Sir Isaac Newton's great contribution to scientific thinking

D. The title of that song by John Lennon

24. Who wrote 'When Britain Really Ruled The Waves'?

A. Gilbert O'Sullivan

B. Gilbert and Sullivan

C. Walt Disney

D. Tim Rice and Andrew Lloyd Webber

Find the answers to this test on p.216.

**'The British public has
always had an unerring taste
for ungifted amateurs.'**

John Osborne

1. What does Eid ul-Adha celebrate?

A. The end of the annual harvest

B. The Prophet Ibrahim being prepared to sacrifice
his son at God's request

C. The end of the fast of Ramadan

D. The Muslim New Year

2. An Anglo-Saxon king is buried at Sutton Hoo in Suffolk. He is remarkable because:

A. He was buried in his ship with his treasure

B. He was buried standing up and holding his sword in a
fighting stance

C. He was buried in a chariot along with his horse
Egbert

D. He was buried with his servants and pet wolf
Dogbert

3. What does 'the Dunkirk spirit' refer to?

A. The tot of rum given to sailors during the evacuation of Dunkirk

B. The resolve in adversity shown during the evacuation of Dunkirk

C. The cheap fuel used by small boats to reach Dunkirk

D. The name of one of the fishing boats which assisted the evacuation

4. What was the Government of Wales Act (1998) about?

A. Welsh MPs could vote on English matters

B. Wales united with England

C. Wales was conquered by England and English laws imposed

D. Wales got its own parliament

> **'When asked his opinion of Welsh nationalism, Mr Thomas replied in three words, two of which were "Welsh nationalism".'**
>
> *Dylan Thomas*

5. TRUE or FALSE: The first Archbishop of Canterbury was a Roman.

6. Nineteenth-century engineer Isambard Kingdom Brunel did NOT build which ONE of the following:

A. Clifton Suspension Bridge

B. Preston Bypass

C. Great Western Railway

D. Thames Tunnel

7. When is the electoral register updated?

A. Every September or October

B. In every election year

C. Every time a new person registers in real-time

D. Every ten years

8. What is the name of the head of the Assembly of the Church of Scotland?

A. Archbishop of Scotland

B. Archbishop of Perth

C. The Moderator

D. The Tulchan

9. What is Baroness Tanni Grey-Thompson famous for?

A. She is a Paralympian holding 11 Paralympic gold medals

B. She is a human rights lawyer who headed the European Court of Human Rights

C. She is owner of Stafford Castle and head of the National Trust

D. She is the head of the British Olympic Committee

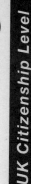

10. Why is the House of Commons regarded as the most important chamber of Parliament?

A. It controls the Armed Forces

B. Its members are elected by the people

C. It has spectacular river views

D. Its members are younger and better educated than the Lords

11. Who was Sir John Millais?

A. A French nineteenth-century painter known for his paintings of peasants

B. A member of the 1966 England World Cup-winning squad

C. A member of Captain Scott's Arctic expedition

D. One of the Pre-Raphaelite Brotherhood

12. Which country is not part of the Commonwealth?

A. Rwanda

B. Cameroon

C. Mozambique

D. Ireland

13. German-speaking King George I needed much ministerial help. His most senior minister became known as:

A. The prime minister

B. The first minister

C. The kaiser

D. The home secretary

14. What happened during the Highland Clearances?

A. Small Scottish farms were destroyed to make way for large flocks of sheep and herds of cattle

B. The Highlands were cleared of trees and undergrowth to facilitate Munro bagging

C. A glut of Scottish whisky was sold off cheap to the French

D. Hikers and ramblers took part in a mass litter-picking exercise to preserve the Scottish landscape

15. What was a central belief of the Enlightenment?

A. That electricity should be available for all

B. That freedom of religious and political belief was a human right

C. That there should be free education for all

D. That women should have the same rights as men

16. Why did the Spanish Armada attack England in 1588?

A. To restore Catholicism to England

B. Nostradamus predicted 1588 would be a year of Spanish glory.

C. To restore Catherine of Aragon as queen

D. To help the Scots fight against Elizabeth I

17. *A Young Person's Guide to the Orchestra* is:

A. A Ladybird book by Sir Simon Rattle

B. A piece of music by Benjamin Britten

C. A TV series first broadcast on BBC2

D. A twelve-week course run by the National Symphony Orchestra

'Because I'm an Englishman I have spent my life in a constant state of embarrassment.'

Colin Firth

18. Which is NOT a responsibility of an elected MP?

A. Think up new laws

B. Criticize and carp about what the government does

C. Represent lobbyists' views in the chamber for a fee

D. Deal with constituents' complaints

19. TRUE or FALSE: The traditional Northern Irish meal the 'Ulster fry' involves two types of pudding and two types of bread.

20. A non-UK national seeking work in the UK can obtain a National Insurance number from:

A. The Department for Work and Pensions

B. Nowhere – they are not entitled to one

C. The Home Office

D. Their local council

21. Which of these terms is the odd one out?

A. Dibbly-dobbly

B. Sticky wicket

C. Shot to nothing

D. Cow corner

'I want to play cricket; it doesn't seem to matter if you win or lose.'

Meat Loaf

22. What is Ernest Rutherford known for?

A. He flew the plane that dropped the first atomic bomb on Japan

B. He split the atom, which led to the development of the atomic bomb

C. He was a British screen actor in the 1940s

D. He campaigned against the use of nuclear weapons

23. Why was Queen Mary known as Bloody Mary?

A. She liked to watch beheadings

B. She persecuted Protestants

C. She introduced an alcoholic drink made from fermented tomatoes

D. Her father Henry VIII gave her the nickname because she was so stubborn

24. What is *Passport to Pimlico*?

A. An internal travel document required for entry into this area of London. It becomes mandatory after Brexit.

B. A cocktail

C. A film

D. A secret code phrase given to new MPs entering the House of Commons

Find the answers to this test on p.220.

> '**Visitors to British hotels will realize**
> *Fawlty Towers* **was really a documentary.**'
> *Lonely Planet Guide to Britain*

1. TV and radio channels ensure rival political views are allotted equal time because:

A. The people in charge believe in giving a balanced view of both sides

B. The viewers and listeners will complain if they don't

C. It is illegal for them not to

D. 'British fair play' is item one on the broadcast charter

2. Charles I made the Scots angry by attempting to do what in 1640?

A. Put a tax on whisky

B. Impose a revised Prayer Book on the Scots

C. Take Edinburgh castle as his home

D. Impose unification between the two countries

3. What was the population of Britain in 1600?

A. One million

B. Four million

C. Ten million

D. Twelve million

4. What is the name of a Sikh place of worship?

A. Temple

B. Quacken

C. Basadi

D. Gurdwara

5. What is notable about David Weir's seven victories at the London marathon?

A. He achieved them all dressed as different Disney characters

B. He achieved them on performance-enhancing drugs

C. He raised a world record amount for charity

D. He achieved them all in a wheelchair

6. Which Anglo-Saxon king defeated the Vikings?

A. Aethelbert

B. Englebert

C. Alfred the Great

D. Egbert the Dane Slayer

'The Italians have got opera, the Spanish have got flamenco dancing. What have we got? Weight Watchers.'

Victoria Wood

7. Where did the game of golf originate?

A. At the court of Henry VIII

B. Fourteenth-century Wales

C. Fifteenth-century Scotland

D. Colonial America in the seventeenth century

8. Which of the following is NOT a criminal offence under British law?

A. Carrying a knife

B. Buying or selling ecstasy

C. Smoking in a public place

D. Discrimination in the workplace

9. Give TWO reasons *Life in the UK* recommends making friends with your neighbours:

A. They might share parking spaces

B. They might feed your pets when you are away

C. They might offer advice on local shops

D. They might invite you round for a barbecue

10. TRUE or FALSE: Adult citizens of the USA, the Commonwealth and the EU resident in the UK can vote in a General Election.

11. Which ONE legacy did the Romans not leave behind in Britain after their 400-year stay?

A. Public roads

B. Public buildings

C. Christianity

D. Alimentum

12. TRUE or FALSE: Under British law, a man who forces a woman to have sex cannot be charged with rape if the woman is his own wife.

13. The Industrial Revolution was made possible by machines driven by:

A. Oil

B. Steam

C. Horsepower

D. Manpower

14. What was the effect of the Statute of Rhuddlan in 1284?

A. Wales was annexed to England

B. Wales became independent from England

C. Wales agreed to unite with England

D. Welsh taxes were collected for the first time

15. Who were the enemy of the English in the Hundred Years War?

A. The Irish

B. The Spanish

C. The French

D. The Scots

> **'Don't trust any Englishman who speaks with a French accent.'**
>
> *French proverb*

16. Which TWO territories did the East India Company control in the nineteenth century?

A. East Indies

B. East Africa

C. India

D. Singapore

17. Where was the first modern tennis club in the world founded?

A. Wimbledon

B. Harrogate

C. Leamington Spa

D. Manchester

18. TRUE or FALSE: Members of the Armed Forces cannot stand for public office.

19. How many members of a jury are there in a Scottish Sheriff Court?

A. Three

B. Ten

C. Twelve

D. Fifteen

20. Who wrote the march for the coronation of Elizabeth II?

A. Sir William Walton

B. Sir Edward Elgar

C. Andrew Lloyd Webber

D. Ralph Vaughan Williams

21. What did the 1957 Treaty of Rome establish?

A. NATO (North Atlantic Treaty Organization)

B. EEC (European Economic Community)

C. G7 (Group of Seven)

D. WTO (World Trade Organization)

22. Name TWO foreign-born painters who were based in Britain:

A. Hans Holbein the Younger

B. Anthony van Dyck

C. J. M. W. Turner

D. Rembrandt van Rijn

23. What are the *Canterbury Tales* about?

A. The history of the Archbishops of Canterbury

B. The adventures of a group making a pilgrimage to Canterbury

C. The life of Thomas Becket

D. A medieval tourist guide to Canterbury

T
E
S
T

10

24. What information can be found in the Domesday Book?

A. A list of all those killed at the battle of Hastings, their wealth (including chickens) and next of kin

B. A list of all those due for execution for resisting Norman rule

C. A list of all those resident in every English town and village after the Norman Conquest, plus their animals

D. William the Conqueror's bill of rights for his new English subjects

'If you want to outwit an Englishman, touch him when he doesn't want to be touched.'

Julian Barnes

Find the answers to this test on p.224.

'We are rigid and formal in
some ways, but we believe in the
right to eccentricity, as long as
the eccentricities are large
enough . . . Woe betide you if
you hold your knife incorrectly,
but good luck to you if you wear
a loincloth and live up a tree.'

Louis de Bernières

1. Which of the following British actors have won Oscars?

A. Dame Judi Dench

B. Sir Anthony Hopkins

C. Colin Firth

D. Daniel Craig

2. TRUE or FALSE: Henry VIII took the title King of Ireland in 1541 after the Irish people invited him to be their monarch.

3. Where did the first Viking raiders come from?

A. Denmark and Norway

B. Sweden and Finland

C. Iceland

D. Greenland

4. TRUE or FALSE: The Normans conquered the whole of Britain.

> **'Class is the British language.'**
>
> *William Golding*

5. What was the name of the British plane capable of vertical take-off and landing?

A. Spitfire

B. Virgin Galactic

C. Harrier

D. Tornado

6. What happened at the Battle of Bannockburn in 1314?

A. England eonquered Scotland

B. Scotland conquered England

C. Scotland defeated the English to remain independent

D. After a stalemate, England and Scotland united

7. How does voting in an election in Northern Ireland differ from elsewhere in the UK?

A. You must get to your polling station before 11 a.m.

B. You must hand in a new voter registration form at the polling station

C. You must show photo ID before voting

D. You must bring your own pencil into the voting booth

8. What was the basis of feudalism?

A. The king ruled absolutely

B. The king appointed lords who in turn appointed committees of local subjects

C. Powerful lords paid fees ('feuds') for the king's lands

D. The king gave lands to his lords; in return, they provided peasant soldiers for his wars

9. Which of the following films was directed by British film-maker David Lean?

A. *A Room with a View*

B. *Brief Encounter*

C. *Mamma Mia*

D. *This is England*

16. Northern Ireland and Scotland have their own banknotes which are:

A. Valid everywhere in Britain, but shops and businesses are not obliged to accept them

B. Valid everywhere in Britain, and shops and businesses must accept them

C. Not valid outside Northern Ireland or Scotland

D. Valid everywhere and must be accepted, but change does not have to be offered

17. The period of Charles II's accession to the throne became known as:

A. The Glorious Revolution

B. The Restoration

C. The Reestablishment

D. The Reformation

'The English do small things well and big things badly.'

Paul Theroux

18. What does Habeas Corpus represent?

A. The right to a proper burial

B. The right to a fair trial

C. The right to free health care

D. The right to marital sexual relations

19. TRUE or FALSE: A constitutional monarchy means the Queen appoints the government

20. William Wilberforce is significant because:

A. He campaigned against the slave trade

B. He was a slave trader who helped build Bristol and Liverpool

C. He was the first freed slave to enter Parliament

D. He employed the first freed slaves and taught them English customs

21. What is the official report of activity in the Houses of Parliament called?

A. Chilcot

B. Hansard

C. Mallard

D. Dullard

22. The Crimean War (1853–56) was fought between:

A. Britain, France and Turkey against Russia

B. Britain against France

C. Britain and France against Crimea

D. Russia and Britain against Turkey

23. Name ONE country that was NOT a British ally in the First World War:

A. Japan

B. Russia

C. Italy

D. Bulgaria

24. What is the difference between the Belfast Agreement and the Good Friday Agreement?

A. The Belfast Agreement provides for the eventual union of Ireland by 2050

B. The Belfast Agreement allows Republicans to bear arms in that city

C. The Belfast Agreement was the precursor to the Good Friday Agreement

D. There is no difference

Find the answers to this test on p.228.

'We may be a small country, but we are a nation of Shakespeare, Churchill, the Beatles, Sean Connery, Harry Potter, David Beckham's right foot . . . David Beckham's left foot, come to that.'

Love, Actually

QUESTIONS
Section 2: Order Of Merit Level

OK, so now you've passed the British citizenship test. But just because you think you know whether the milk or tea goes in first (according to Debrett's, the correct way is the tea first, and 'don't hold your little finger in the air'), that doesn't mean you can get on your high horse. The following 11 tests are NOT based on the *Life in the UK* handbook. They have been compiled with a view to weeding out the hoi polloi, the common people, and narrowing it down to the elite (or hoi oligoi if you want to get all Ancient Greek about it). An exclusive club for those in the know. Just like it used to be, back in the day. The day when Britannia ruled the waves, the day of the Empire on which the sun never set.

Do you want to join that club? Do you know the highly eccentric provisions of the 1986 Salmon Act? Or why the Exchequer is called the Exchequer? The rules, regulations and cultural quirks of life in Britain can be odd, baffling and sometimes downright bonkers. If you can keep your head when all about you are losing theirs, if you can answer these questions with a confident shrug, you can count yourself as a member of that most exclusive of clubs – you'll be a Brit, my son.*

* Or indeed daughter.

> '[An Englishman] does everything on principle: he fights you on patriotic principles; he robs you on business principles; he enslaves you on imperial principles.'
>
> *George Bernard Shaw*

T E S T 1

1. 'The Forme of Cury' is one of the UK's oldest collections of recipes dating from around 1390. It shows how to prepare what?

A. Curry

B. Dodo

C. Whale

D. Human tongue

2. True or False: It is illegal to be drunk in a British pub.

3. The Queen's Diamond Jubilee State Coach is stuffed with artefacts from British history. Name ONE relic that is NOT included:

A. Wood from Henry VIII's ship *Mary Rose*

B. A model of the double-helix structure of DNA identified by Crick and Watson

C. A musketball from the Battle of Waterloo

D. Wood from the apple tree Sir Isaac Newton sat under

4. If a child is born on a flight from London to LA, how will their passport record their place of birth?

A. 'London'

B. 'LA'

C. 'Holder Born on an Aeroplane'

D. 'Mid-Air Birth' followed by longitude and latitude map reference of the birth

5. Who are genetically the 'most British' people in the UK?

A. People from Lancashire

B. People from Yorkshire

C. Londoners

D. People from Cornwall

6. How is Napoleon Bonaparte reputed to have described the English?

A. A nation of shopkeepers

B. A nation of shoppers

C. A nation of drinkers

D. A nation of '*rosbifs*'

> **'The English have no exalted sentiments. They can all be bought.'**
> *Napoleon Bonaparte*

7. The Angevin Empire – what was it?

A. Queen Victoria's favourite horse, which won the Derby in 1893

B. The lands on the Continent ruled by English kings in the twelfth and thirteenth centuries

C. The fictitious alien empire in H. G. Wells' *War of the Worlds*

D. The Welsh cinema which showed the first moving pictures in 1889

8. The codebreakers at Bletchley Park during the Second World War were recruited through:

A. Recommendations from the Faculty of Mathematics of Cambridge University

B. An ad in *The Times*

C. A crossword puzzle in the *Daily Telegraph*

D. Candidates put forward by the Oxford Professor of Mathematics

9. TRUE or FALSE: *Coronation Street* is the longest-running programme on British TV.

10. In the eighteenth century, you could be transported to a penal colony in Australia and subjected to hard labour if you stole:

A. A napkin

B. A side of bacon

C. A ribbon

D. An orange

11. What was the 1986 Salmon Act?

A. It outlawed any one person eating more than three portions of wild salmon per head a week

B. Proposed by SNP's Alex Salmond, it set the stage for an eventual devolution of powers for Scotland

C. It made it illegal to handle a salmon in suspicious circumstances

D. It made it illegal to catch and keep salmon weighing over 10 lb

12. At what age can a UK child legally start babysitting?

A. 12

B. 14

C. 16

D. 18

> **'It was revealed in a government survey published today that the prime minister is doing the work of two men, Laurel and Hardy.'**
>
> *Ronnie Corbett*

13. Which TWO of the following species are all the property of the Queen?

A. Porpoises

B. Corgis

C. Whales

D. Horses

14. Where is same-sex marriage still illegal in the UK?

A. The Armed Services

B. Gibraltar

C. Northern Ireland

D. Isle of Man

15. TRUE or FALSE: A British prime minister has never been assassinated.

16. The Royal Mint introduced a new plastic £5 note in 2017 which proved controversial because:

A. People complained that the texture was too slippery

B. There was an outcry about having a picture of Jane Austen on the back

C. Vegetarians were angry because it contained animal tallow

D. The Queen felt it made her profile look too old

17. In the 1930s, a *Times* headline is supposed to have reported: 'Fog in the Channel. Continent cut off.' What was the German response?

A. 'We must do our utmost to preserve the tremendous British sense of humour once we invade.'

B. 'Why is this amusing? This is a silly joke and not logical.'

C. 'We see the absurdity of a small island imagining itself so important that the Continent should be isolated from it.'

D. 'This fog which the British find so amusing will provide cover for our glorious and irreversible invasion.'

18. In the event of a devastating attack on the UK mainland, alleged secret instructions for Royal Navy nuclear submarines patrolling the world's oceans are to listen out for:

A. The BBC World Service

B. Radio 4's *Today* programme

C. *The Archers*

D. A broadcast message from the prime minister or the Queen

> '**Even though they probably certainly
> know that you probably wouldn't,
> they don't certainly know that
> although you probably wouldn't,
> there is no probability that you
> certainly would!**'
>
> *Sir Humphrey Appleby* explaining the
> nuclear deterrent in *Yes, Prime Minister*

19. A 2016 UNICEF Fairness for Children report ranked the world's richest 37 countries in terms of the achievement gap between low-achieving children and the average child in reading, maths and science at the age of 15. Where did the UK rank?

A. 1st

B. 37th

C. 10th

D. 25th

20. Nineteenth-century British prime minister Lord Salisbury pursued a policy of 'splendid isolation'. What did it mean?

A. Keeping Britain at a distance from all foreign entanglements

B. Lord Salisbury was not to be disturbed, so he could govern without distraction

C. Keeping Britain at arm's length from France and Germany

D. Keeping Britain at a distance from Russia

21. How far do British territorial waters extend from the coast?

A. 1 mile

B. 5 miles

C. 12 miles

D. 100 miles

22. Where does the expression 'small beer' originate?

A. A pre-metric measurement in pubs

B. A corruption of the Viking spelling of 'small bear', which they hunted

C. The low-alcohol beer which was generally drunk by all in Britain, including children, from medieval times onwards

D. Victorian Cockney rhyming slang for cheap ale (not dear/small beer)

23. Before he formulated his theory of evolution, Charles Darwin intended to be:

A. A singer

B. A priest

C. A teacher

D. A politician

24. Which of the following towns has NOT been a capital city?

A. Winchester

B. Colchester

C. Tamworth

D. Bath

'After thousands of years of confused immigrants putting too much Marmite on their toast or serving pints of beer almost two-thirds full, the government finally got round to producing a booklet outlining a few basics. *Life in the UK* is the official guide to British idiosyncrasies for those trying to make some sense of the cold, wet country they hope to make their home.'

John O'Farrell

Find the answers to this test on p.234.

Section 2: Test 2

**'If it is good to have one foot in England,
it is still better, or at least as good,
to have the other out of it.'**

Henry James

1. Which of the following ranks highest in a list of the most educated regions of the UK?

A. Oxfordshire, Bucks and Berks

B. Inner London East

C. North-east Scotland

D. Outer London South

2. If you own land or property in the UK, how far underground do your ownership rights extend?

A. 100 metres

B. 10 meters

C. Down to the earth's core

D. 1 mile

3. Where do men have the longest life expectancy in the UK?

A. Glasgow

B. London

C. Sussex

D. Dorset

4. Where is underage pregnancy most common in the UK?

A. Nuneaton

B. Preston

C. Norwich

D. Blackpool

5. Who was the greatest Briton after Churchill and Isambard Kingdom Brunel, according to a 2002 BBC national poll?

A. Sir Isaac Newton

B. William Shakespeare

C. Charles Darwin

D. Diana, Princess of Wales

'Life is unliveable to them [the English] unless they have tea and puddings.'
George Orwell

6. If you receive a 'threp in't steans' in Yorkshire, what should you do?

A. Ring the fire brigade

B. Seek medical attention

C. Check your mortgage details

D. Summon friends for a celebratory barbecue

7. How should you first address the Queen?

A. Ma'am

B. Your Majesty

C. Your Royal Highness

D. Your excellency

8. In the mid 1990s, Tory MP Jonathan Aitken vowed to 'cut out the cancer of bent and twisted journalism' by taking the *Guardian* and Granada TV to court for libel. What was the ultimate outcome?

A. Aitken was awarded £1 million damages

B. Aitken was sentenced to 18 months in prison

C. Alan Rusbridger, the *Guardian* editor, was sentenced to 18 months in prison

D. The case was settled out of court

9. 'Is it a book you would wish your wife or servants to read?' Which book was prosecuting lawyer Mervyn Griffith-Jones talking about in a famous obscenity trial?

A. *Fifty Shades of Grey* by E. L. James

B. *Lady Chatterley's Lover* by D. H. Lawrence

C. *The Book of Lies* by Aleister Crowley

D. *Venus in the Cloister or the Nun in her Smock* by Edward Curll

10. Reebok is a British sports shoe company. Why is it named after a South African deer?

A. The founder is half South African

B. They use deer leather in their shoes

C. The founder saw the name in a dictionary and liked it

D. The factory is in South Africa

11. What debt do we owe the actors John Heminges and Henry Condell?

A. They were the stuntmen in many 007 films

B. They were body doubles Winston Churchill used to fool the Nazis in the Second World War

C. They founded the famous acting school RADA

D. They made Shakespeare popular by publishing his plays

12. Harrods installed the first escalator in 1898. What were customers offered when they reached the top?

A. A glass of champagne

B. A certificate of travel

C. Brandy or smelling salts

D. Counselling

Q. Why don't the British panic?
A. They do, but very quietly. It is impossible for the naked eye to tell their panic from their ecstasy.

George Mikes

13. What was the first book published in English?

A. The King James Bible

B. Chaucer's *Canterbury Tales*

C. *Dictes and Sayinges of the Philosophres*

D. *Sir Gawain and the Green Knight*

14. Where was Archibald Leach, who became a Hollywood film legend, born?

A. Bristol

B. Sheffield

C. Scunthorpe

D. Austin, Texas

15. The Freedom of Information Act was passed in 2000. Tony Blair later described it as:

A. 'A shining example of British democracy in action'

B. 'My proudest achievement in domestic politics'

C. 'One of the biggest mistakes of my career'

D. 'Like handing over the keys to the sweet shop'

16. Which of the following was NOT taxed in the eighteenth century?

A. Cats

B. Gloves

C. Hats

D. Wallpaper

> **'In England, we have come to rely upon a comfortable time-lag of 50 years or a century intervening between the perception that something ought to be done and a serious attempt to do it.'**
>
> *H. G. Wells*

17. What's the bingo lingo for 71?

A. Bang on the drum

B. This is such fun

C. Band on the run

D. Shooting the Hun

18. What is the most commonly spoken language in England and Wales after English?

A. Urdu

B. Punjabi

C. Arabic

D. Polish

19. What was the code name for the German invasion plan of the UK in 1940?

A. Operation Oscar

B. Operation Sea Lion

C. Case Yellow

D. Plan White

20. The CIA are known to give which British product to Taliban warlords as a bribe?

A. Scotch Whisky

B. Viagra

C. Cheddar cheese

D. Rolls Royce cars

21. What was Ian Fleming's inspiration for the name James Bond?

A. Brooke Bond tea

B. Premium bonds

C. An American ornithologist called James Bond

D. Mayfair's Bond Street

22. Where do the Martians land in H. G. Wells' *War of the Worlds*?

A. St James' Park, London

B. Woking, Surrey

C. Erdington, Birmingham

D. Longsight, Manchester

23. According to an Ipsos MORI poll commissioned by Channel 4 in in 2013 about what it means to be British, people were most proud of:

A. The Royal Family

B. Britain's history

C. The NHS

D. The Armed Forces

24. Of every 100 people of working age, how many are unemployed and looking for work?

A. 4.5

B. 14

C. 22.5

D. 11

Find the answers to this test on p.239.

Section 2: Test 3

**'The funniest thing of all is that
even if you love England and belong to
it, you still can't make head or tail of it.'**

G. K. Chesterton

1. What mistake did Laurence Olivier make when portraying Admiral Horatio Nelson in *That Hamilton Woman* in 1941?

A. He tucked his empty left sleeve away, not his right

B. He wore an eyepatch

C. He did not attempt to disguise the fact that he was
a foot taller than Nelson

D. He spoke in crisp RP whereas Nelson had a broad
West Country accent

2. GMT is Greenwich Mean Time. What is Sandringham Time?

A. The predecessor of GMT, dictated by an atomic clock kept in
the Queen's bedroom at Sandringham

B. The time at Sandringham, where clocks were set half an hour
later than the rest of the country

C. Royal slang for the monarch's annual three-week stay on her
Norfolk estate

D. The Queen Mother's way of complaining about slow service at
Sandringham (e.g. 'Where is my G&T? These people work on
Sandringham time.')

3. According to Section 60, subsection 3 of the 1854 Metropolitan Police Act, which is still in force, a £500 fine can be imposed for:

A. Beating a doormat in the street after 8 a.m.

B. Beating a carpet in the street at any time

C. Beating a child in the street after 6 p.m.

D. Beating your wife in the street after 6 p.m.

4. The Auld Alliance of 1295 was a pact between which countries and for what purpose?

A. England and Scotland would come to each other's aid if attacked by France

B. Scotland and France would come to each other's aid if attacked by England

C. Scotland and Ireland would unite to fight Wales

D. Scotland and Wales would join forces against Ireland

5. What is the fundamental principle behind British scientist James Lovelock's Gaia theory?

A. Global warming can be halted if we ban all cars now

B. The Environmental Apocalypse is inevitable and the world will end soon

C. That life on earth regulates its own environment

D. Cannabis should be legalized to reduce human stress

6. TRUE or FALSE: A husband and wife cannot be prosecuted for conspiracy to commit a crime

7. What is the name of the Queen's tiara on British coins?

A. The Queen Mary Circlet

B. The Boys and Girls of Great Britain Tiara

C. The Girls of Great Britain and Ireland Tiara

D. The Imperial Diadem

8. Which of the following truly originated in Britain?

A. St George

B. Teabag

C. Pubs

D. Fish 'n' chips

> **'If I had to choose between betraying my country and betraying my friend, I hope I should have the guts to betray my country.'**
>
> *E. M. Forster*

9. What is the average annual cost of educating an English secondary state school pupil?

A. £3,550

B. £4,550

C. £9,550

D. £12,550

10. Eton College was established in 1440 by Henry VI with the aim of educating:

A. Choristers and priests for the church

B. Sons of the King's barons

C. Poor boys

D. Sons of the King's knights and men at arms

> 'British education is probably the best in the world, if you can survive it. If you can't, there is nothing left for you but the diplomatic corps.'
>
> *Peter Ustinov*

11. The first English dictionary *A Table Alphabeticall of Hard Words* was published in 1604. How many words did it contain?

A. 2,543

B. 10,505

C. 5,601

D. 32,678

12. Visitors to Oxford's Bodleian Library must take an oral oath. It includes a promise not to:

A. Handle the books with bloodstained hands

B. Use any ideas from library books to foment violent dissent or revolution

C. Bring any form of alcohol into the library

D. Bring fire or flame into the library

13. The Beatles appeared on the *Morecambe and Wise Show* in 1963. What name did Eric Morecambe call Ringo Starr?

A. Richard

B. Bonzo

C. Bongo

D. John

14. Who was first to crack Enigma codes used by the Nazis during the Second World War?

A. Jim Sanborn for the CIA

B. Three Polish mathematicians

C. Alan Turing in Milton Keynes

D. Benedict Cumberbatch

15. In Britain, which is the furthest place from the sea?

A. Bradford, Yorkshire

B. Kettering, Northamptonshire

C. Church Flatts Farm, Derbyshire

D. Banbury, Oxfordshire

'The English man-in-the-street is largely envious, vindictive and punitive. It is a mercy that there aren't more referendums in this country. They would be hanging children.'

Jeffrey Bernard

16. The Norwegian Storegga Slides were a series of landslides which deeply affected Britain because:

A. They triggered a tsunami which made Britain an island

B. They created a land bridge which brought the mammoth to Britain

C. They wiped out the woolly mammoth in northern Europe

D. They created the Lake District

17. What qualifications does the Queen have?

A. Five O levels

B. Seven O levels

C. None

D. BA (Hons) from Durham University

18. ***Protect and Survive*** **was a government advice leaflet issued in the 1980s. It told the UK population what to do in the event of a nuclear attack. What did it suggest?**

A. Build a shelter in a cupboard under the stairs

B. Get out into the open as far away as possible from buildings

C. Duck and cover, put your head between your legs, and kiss your ass goodbye

D. Find the nearest government nuclear shelter

19. **TRUE or FALSE:** The average Briton is 20 per cent Franco-German.

'Put three Englishmen on a desert island and within an hour they'll have invented a class system.'

Alan Ayckbourn

20. **Which of these countries consumes the most wine?**

A. Great Britain

B. Germany

C. France

D. America

21. TRUE or FALSE: A special terminal is set up at Heathrow for the exclusive use of royalty and VIPs.

22. Is there anything British left behind on the moon?

A. No

B. Union Jack graffiti scratched onto the lunar module

C. A King James Bible left behind by Buzz Aldrin

D. The lunar rover designed by Rolls Royce

23. 'Duty of care' became a legal concept in the UK in 1932 because:

A. A woman found a snail in her ginger beer while visiting a café in Scotland

B. The care of elderly relatives had become a big issue for the electorate

C. There was an outcry over the plight of disabled veterans from the First World War

D. A man was hit by falling masonry at a hotel in the West Country

24. What does 'bagging a Munro' mean?

A. Buying a stash of heroin from your dealer

B. Wrapping a fried Mars bar up in a chip shop

C. Climbing a Scottish mountain

D. Putting uneaten haggis in a doggy bag for later

Find the answers to this test on p.244.

Find the answers to this test on p.244.

'I like a man to be a clean, strong, upstanding Englishman who can look his gnu in the face and put an ounce of lead in it.'

P. G. Wodehouse

1. In 2013, what did the UK Public Accounts Committee describe as one of the worst fiascos ever?

A. The purchase of Royal Navy aircraft carriers with faulty engines

B. The construction of the Scottish Parliament building

C. The bulk order of leaking biros for the civil service

D. An NHS computer system failure

2. Which citizens are most likely to feel discriminated against due to their accent?

A. Scousers

B. Brummies

C. Cockneys

D. Weegies

3. In 2014, Facebook bought a small Somerset research company. What did they ask them to create?

A. A solar-powered plane that could stay airborne for three months

B. A genetically engineered cow to produce low-fat cream

C. A secret new virtual-reality app

D. A hot-air balloon which could circumnavigate the globe

4. The UK's accidentally damaged banknotes service processes more than £100,000 worth of claims each year. The most damage is caused by:

A. Banknotes ruined in the wash

B. Banknotes chewed by a pet

C. Banknotes ripped accidentally

D. Banknotes stained by cocaine

5. NASA's *Voyager I* spacecraft, launched in 1977, is now 12 billion miles from Earth. It contains music for alien civilizations to enjoy. The Beatles' 'Here Comes The Sun' was not included because:

A. NASA only included classical music

B. EMI refused to grant permission for use of the song

C. NASA chose to include the Beatles' 'All Across The Universe' instead

D. The reference to the sun would give away our position to potentially aggressive aliens

6. In the sixteenth century, a London law forbade a man to beat his wife:

A. After 9 p.m.

B. With a stick wider than a man's little finger and longer than his forearm

C. Unless she had been unfaithful

D. Unless she had insulted his beard

> **'It is illegal in England to state in print that a wife can and should derive pleasure from intercourse.'**
>
> *Bertrand Russell*

7. What advice does Rudyard Kipling's poem 'If' give in regard to someone hating you?

A. Make allowance for them

B. Delete them from your Christmas card list

C. Ask them why

D. Don't give way to hating

8. What did Lord Uxbridge lose at the Battle of Waterloo?

A. An arm

B. A horse

C. A leg

D. A watch

9. What is 'Rule, Britannia!' actually about?

A. A patriotic ode to the British monarchy

B. A rebellious cry against the King for not attacking the Spanish

C. An appeal against slavery

D. A satire on Charles Parnell's Home Rule for Ireland

10. The Contagious Diseases Act of 1864 stipulated:

A. Men and women with venereal disease be given free treatment

B. Women with venereal disease be arrested and detained for up to a year

C. Prostitution be made illegal

D. Men and women with venereal disease be transported to an Australian penal colony

11. In 1877, British women's campaigner Anne Besant published an American physician's book, *Fruits of Philosophy: The Private Companion of Young Married People*. It caused a scandal. Why?

A. It suggested different sexual positions

B. It suggested methods of contraception

C. It advocated free love and swapping partners with other young married couples

D. It was the first photographic pornography

Q

> 'Continental people have
> sex lives; the English have
> hot water bottles.'
>
> *George Mikes*

12. In 2017, MPs warned of vigilantes using firearms on British streets against:

A. ISIS sympathizers

B. Chuggers (charity muggers)

C. Mobile phone thieves on mopeds

D. Seagulls

13. The brass letterbox on the front door of 10 Downing Street bears the inscription:

A. 'Prime Minister of Great Britain'

B. 'Her Majesty's Cabinet'

C. 'First Lord of the Treasury'

D. 'Property of the Crown'

14. Why was the classic 1970s ITV cop series starring John Thaw called *The Sweeney*?

A. He played DI Jack Sweeney

B. The Sweeney was the south London boozer where he met informants

C. The Sweeney is slang for the police department featured in the series

D. The Sweeney is slang for 'the boss'

15. The SAS and SBS are UK 'Special Forces' regiments. What is E Squadron?

A. The weakest regiment, i.e. after A B, C and D

B. The elite of the elite, drawn from all Special Forces

C. Escape Squadron, used for hostage extraction

D. Execution Squadron, used for assassinations

16. Which of the following errors or anachronisms does NOT appear in any of Shakespeare's plays?

A. Milan and Verona portrayed as ports when they are not near the sea

B. Ancient Egyptians playing billiards when the game was not yet invented

C. Romans in Caesar's time consulting clocks a thousand years too early

D. Wessex owning a tobacco plantation in America

17. In the event of a successful German invasion, Churchill proposed:

A. Peaceful negotiation

B. Suicide bombing

C. Surrendering south of Watford

D. Offering the Germans Scotland

18. What's the average time a murderer sentenced to life imprisonment spends in prison in the UK?

A. 17 years

B. Life

C. 25 years

D. 10 years

19. What is Scottish con artist Arthur Furguson reputed to have done in the 1920s?

A. Enjoyed a State visit to France posing as the Prince of Wales

B. Dined with the King at Buckingham Palace posing as the German ambassador

C. Sold Nelson's Column to a tourist

D. Won £100,000 by cheating in the *QE2*'s casino and escaping in a lifeboat

20. TRUE or FALSE: Orkney and Shetland were seized from Norway in battle.

21. On average, what percentage of the year does a UK car remain parked?

A. 52 per cent

B. 68 per cent

C. 72 per cent

D. 96 per cent

22. What did banker Nick Leeson say after causing the collapse of Barings, Britain's oldest investment bank, in 1995?

A. 'I'm the fall guy. I only blew £200 million.'

B. 'My ego wrote a cheque. My ass couldn't cash it.'

C. 'It's only money for God's sake. Nobody died.'

D. 'This is just the start. Bankers are out of control. You wait and see.'

'It used to be a slight hallmark of being English or British that one didn't make a big thing out of patriotic allegiance, and was indeed brimful of sarcastic or critical remarks about the old country, but would pull oneself together and say a word or two if it was attacked or criticized in any nasty or stupid manner by anybody else.'

Christopher Hitchens

23. Whose funeral was the odd one out?

A. Nelson

B. Duke of Wellington

C. Winston Churchill

D. Diana, Princess of Wales

24. You're a footman announcing the arrival of Mrs Featherstonehaugh from Cholmondeley. How do you pronounce her surname and village?

A. 'Mrs Fanshaw from Chumley'

B. 'Mrs Feather-Stone-Whore from Chol-mond-delay'

C. 'Mrs F from up North'

D. 'I'm sorry, I didn't catch your name'

Find the answers to this test on p.249.

> 'What has always puzzled me is why the English, who are so profoundly honest, write the best novels about thieves, crooks and lurid murderers.'
>
> *Elsa Schiaparelli*

1. Why was the Dorset village of Tynham shelled in 1943?

A. To flush out suspected German infiltrators

B. By mistake

C. British Army target practice

D. The villagers refused to provide the troops stationed nearby with tea and cakes.

2. What is the most popular piece of music requested on *Desert Island Discs*?

A. The Beatles' 'Yesterday'

B. Beethoven's Symphony No. 9

C. Mozart's Symphony No. 4

D. The Eagles' 'Hotel California'

3. What is the motto of the Most Honourable Order of the Garter?

A. *Dieu et mon droit*

B. *Honi soit qui mal y pense*

C. *Toujours fidèle*

D. *Ad eundum quo nemo ante iit*

4. Which Westminster Abbey tomb are visitors forbidden to walk on?

A. Sir Isaac Newton's

B. Jane Austen's

C. William Shakespeare's

D. The tomb of the unknown warrior

'Well, you'll be glad to know that scientists have finally explained why we've been enduring this rather long spell of disappointing weather. Apparently . . . we live in Britain.'

Hugh Dennis

5. According to the Köppen Climate Classification, the UK enjoys:

A. A Goldilocks climate: not too hot and not too cold

B. A temperate oceanic climate

C. A rainy, windy and depressing climate

D. A multi-profile high-precipitation climate

6. What action by Lloyds Bank after the 2008 financial crash was described as 'truly shocking conduct'?

A. Its executives accepted large bonuses

B. It invented a new type of fraud

C. It falsified its accounts

D. It retired its famous black horse and hired a black pig

'If we are heartbroken
we don't scream in your
face with tears – we go
home and cry on our own.'

Michael Caine

7. What was achieved at 48 Doughty Street, London W1?

A. Vera Brittain wrote *Testament of Youth*

B. Charles Dickens wrote *Oliver Twist*

C. Amal Clooney became a barrister

D. A. A. Milne wrote *Winnie-the-Pooh*

8. The Coach & Horses pub in London's Soho is a legendary bohemian hang-out. Landlord Norman Balon's memoir is called:

A. *Time, Gentlemen, Please*

B. *One More for the Road*

C. *Give Me a Stiff One*

D. *You're Barred, You Bastards*

9. Which of the following unflattering names have been applied to the British?

A. Les goddams

B. Brittunculi

C. Inselaffe

D. Limey

10. What is the Exchequer?

A. Another name for the head tax office

B. The house where the Chancellor lives

C. The Bank of England department for processing cheques

D. The government department collecting and allocating all revenues

11. Where was the Queen born?

A. Buckingham Palace

B. 17 Bruton Street

C. Clarence House

D. 145 Piccadilly

12. The first recorded toast was given at a feast honouring British King Vortigern by Saxon leader Hengist in 450. A guest cried 'Waes Hael!' What does it mean?

A. Good health!

B. Good appetite!

C. All hail!

D. Why sail? (i.e. you are welcome to stay)

13. TRUE or FALSE: Scouse is a meal.

14. Which was the world's first parliament?

A. The English Parliament

B. The Icelandic parliament

C. The Isle of Man parliament

D. Irish parliament

15. When did Oxford University go co-ed?

A. 1852

B. 1928

C. 1945

D. 1974

16. In Guernsey, who is known as the Duke of Normandy?

A. Jimmy Tarbuck, who has a second home there

B. The Queen

C. Newscaster Moira Stuart, who has a second home there

D. The island's beloved mascot cow

> '[The British] are the only people who like to be told how bad things are, who like to be told the worst.'
>
> *Winston Churchill*

17. What is the largest denomination UK banknote?

A. Fifty pounds

B. One hundred pounds

C. Five hundred pounds

D. One hundred million pounds

18. If you are born on a flight from London to New York, what nationality are you?

A. British

B. American

C. The nationality of the country where the airline on which you are travelling is registered

D. The nationality of your parents

'We're doomed! Doomed I tell you!'

Private Frazer, Dad's Army

19. When a product is labelled By Appointment to Her Majesty the Queen it indicates:

A. That she has shares in the company

B. That it has been supplied to her household for at least five years

C. That the manufacturer donates it free to Her Majesty

D. That she recommends it in return for a fee

20. Which is NOT a duty of the official called Black Rod?

A. Knocking on the door of the Commons

B. Arresting badly behaving Lords

C. Helping the whips to make sure MPs are present for crucial votes

D. Overseeing a £30 million security budget

21. What is the average height of a UK male?

A. 5 foot 9.5 inches (177.6 cm)

B. 5 foot 10 inches (177.8 cm)

C. 5 foot 11 inches (180.3 cm)

D. 6 feet (182.8 cm)

22. What did the British Army abolish in 1916?

A. Execution for desertion

B. Red tunics in favour of camouflage

C. Compulsory moustaches

D. Cavalry charges on horseback

23. Which of the following was a common Elizabethan delicacy?

A. Crane

B. Bustard

C. Swan

D. Stork

24. What is rumoured to be buried alongside poet Edmund Spenser in his Westminster Abbey tomb?

A. Unpublished lines by Shakespeare

B. His gay lover Christopher Marlowe

C. A love letter to Shakespeare's wife Anne Hathaway

D. A confession to the murder of Christopher Marlowe

Find the answers to this test on p.254.

'I know I have but the body of a weak and feeble woman, but I have the heart and stomach of a king, and of a king of England too.'

Elizabeth I

1. Why did Captain Scott write 'The worst has happened' in his diary on 17 January 1912, on his expedition to the South Pole?

A. He was delayed by a snowstorm

B. His support team hadn't turned up

C. Someone else had reached the South Pole first

D. He lost his sleeping bag

2. Where did the modern Olympic games originate?

A. Athens

B. Paris

C. Sparta

D. Shropshire

3. In 1980, £24,000 was:

A. The price of the average UK house

B. The highest prize money for any UK game show

C. The average annual salary for a male professional

D. The highest fee ever paid for a footballer

4. What is known in America as Chateau Snavely?

A. The sitcom *Fawlty Towers*

B. Buckingham Palace

C. Terrible British wine

D. Windsor Castle

5. Why is Dr Andrew Wakefield controversial?

A. He cloned a human baby

B. He suggested a link between the MMR vaccine and autism

C. He said bacon caused cancer

D. He promoted assisted suicide

6. Where is the world's largest British ex-pat population?

A. Spain

B. Canada

C. America

D. Australia

> '**Do you realize that people die of boredom in London suburbs? It's the second biggest cause of death amongst the English in general. Sheer boredom.**'
>
> *Alexander McCall Smith*

7. In 1969, Manchester United paid £204,028 for what?

A. To sign George Best

B. A new stand for Old Trafford

C. Players' wages

D. A new team bus

8. What did Labour MP Tony Benn admit to secretly doing in a House of Commons broom cupboard?

A. Having sex

B. Meeting with a member of the IRA

C. Drunkenly writing 'Sometimes I wish Guy Fawkes had succeeded' on the wall

D. Putting up a plaque in memory of a woman killed by a horse

9. Which of the following was last to become extinct in Britain?

A. Mammoth

B. Woolly rhinoceros

C. Eurasian wolf

D. Brown bear

10. Which of the following has Channel 4 NOT broadcast?

A. A season of banned documentaries

B. A drama about the kidnapping of Prince Harry

C. A week of programmes about masturbation

D. A drama about the execution of Gary Glitter

11. What used to be known as a 'frost fair'?

A. A spectacle of music and dance on ice

B. A fair or market on the River Thames

C. A sale of winter clothing at Harrods opened by the Queen

D. Victorian ice-skating races

'This is the only country in the world where you step on somebody's foot and he apologises.'

Keith Waterhouse

12. What did Samuel Pepys bury in his garden during the Great Fire of London?

A. His life savings

B. His wife

C. Cheese

D. A treasure map

13. Where does the phrase 'the man on the Clapham omnibus' come from?

A. A character played by James Mason in the 1936 film *The Clapham Omnibus*

B. The first market-research survey into London transport in the 1920s

C. A coinage first thought up by Walter Bagehot, a Victorian journalist

D. The often aggressive behaviour of commuters into the City of London at the end of the nineteenth century

14. Why has London been dubbed the 'Global Laundromat'?

A. The British reputation for honesty and fair dealing in the City

B. It is the global centre for trade in industrial detergents

C. More than 1 million Chinese first came to London to work in laundries

D. It is a centre for international money-laundering

15. What is the claim to fame of Rhossili Bay in Wales?

A. It is the scene of the only ever fatal shark attack in British waters

B. BBC series *Poldark* is filmed there

C. Its beach has been voted the best in Europe

D. It is the setting for Tom Jones' 'The Green Green Grass Of Home'

16. Which of the following is current British youth slang meaning 'gorgeous' or 'tasty'?

A. Sick

B. Topping

C. Gnarly

D. Peng

17. What was the name of Tony Blair's rock band at Oxford University?

A. Weapons of Mass Destruction

B. Attention Deficit

C. Ugly Rumours

D. Leftfield

> **'A thin grey fog hung over the city, and the streets were very cold; for summer was in England.'**
>
> *Rudyard Kipling*

18. Who were Homer, Hicks, Stanley and Johnson?

A. The gang members in *A Clockwork Orange*

B. Four British spies

C. Oswald Mosley's henchmen

D. England cricket team members accused of dangerous bowling in the 1926 Ashes series

19. Where does the expression 'by hook or by crook' come from?

A. English privateers, who would use grappling hooks and crooks (hooked staffs) to board enemy vessels

B. Fagin used the term in Charles Dickens' *Oliver Twist*

C. The witches say it in *Macbeth*

D. A medieval bye-law governing the collection of firewood

20. Why was the Queen awarded £369 million by the British government in 2017?

A. To replace the Crown Jewels

B. To cover legal fees resulting from some of the Duke of Edinburgh's public comments

C. To do up her house

D. To fund a replacement for the Royal Yacht *Britannia*

21. Margaret Thatcher had a problem with British Airways in the 1990s. What was it?

A. She didn't like their multicultural livery

B. She didn't like their chicken biryani or the toffee dessert

C. They wouldn't lend her planes during the Falklands War

D. Her son Mark had been turned down as a pilot

22. What is the Chatham House rule?

A. The rules of a country-house murder game which became Cluedo

B. The tradition which began at Chatham House in Kent, whereby port and cigars cannot be served with ladies present

C. A convention whereby what is said in a meeting can be reported as long as it is not attributed to anyone

D. A rule from an early form of tennis whereby players each brought their own umpire

23. Which of the following was NOT used by Allied High Command to draw landing maps for D-Day?

A. Old family snaps from holidays in Normandy

B. Divers creeping ashore to take photos

C. Air reconnaissance

D. Long-range telescopes

24. TRUE or FALSE: The Great Train Robber Ronald Biggs made a record with Brazilian artist Gilberto Gil while on the run in Rio.

Find the answers to this test on p.258.

'Once, when a British Prime Minister sneezed, men half a world away would blow their noses. Now when a British Prime Minister sneezes nobody else will even say, "Bless You."'

Bernard Levin

1. What is the origin and meaning of the word 'druid'?

A. Saxon for 'wizard'

B. Old Norse for 'sage'

C. Celtic for 'knower of the oak'

D. Middle English for 'weirdo'

2. What is the most common pub name in the UK?

A. Queen's Head

B. Black Swan

C. White Hart

D. Red Lion

3. According to Pulp's 'Common People', what do the working class do to alleviate boredom?

A. Fight, steal and sleep

B. Watch TV and eat biscuits

C. Smoke

D. Drink, dance and have sex

4. What happened to John Rennie's London Bridge, built in 1831?

A. It burned down in 1968 and was replaced by the present London Bridge in 1972

B. It was moved to Arizona

C. It fell down and lies at the bottom of the Thames

D. It was demolished, and its stone was used to build the British Museum

5. TRUE or FALSE: Noon GMT is when the sun is at its highest point in the sky.

6. Why was the birth of Louise Joy Brown in Oldham in July 1978 significant?

A. She was the first genetically modified embryo

B. She received the first heart transplant

C. She was the first to receive foetal surgery while still in her mother's womb

D. She was the first test-tube baby

> 'England has two books,
> the Bible and Shakespeare.
> England made Shakespeare,
> but the Bible made England.'
>
> *Victor Hugo*

7. Why was Glenn Hoddle fired as manager of the England football team in 1999?

A. England lost to San Marino and didn't qualify for the World Cup

B. He was caught accepting a bribe

C. He made controversial comments about disabled people

D. He said he wanted Germany to win the World Cup

8. Why is British currency called 'pound sterling'?

A. Sterling comes from the Middle English 'star', a mark for the most valuable coin

B. The Royal Mint was moved to Stirling (Sterling) in Scotland after England and Scotland were joined together under James VI

C. 'Sterling' means 'solid, respectable and fit for purpose', a description that could be applied to the British pound at least until fairly recently

D. It refers to a weight of silver

9. What was Charles II's wife Catherine of Braganza's contribution to the English breakfast?

A. She invented marmalade

B. She introduced it as a formal meal from her native Portugal

C. She popularized tea as a drink

D. She pioneered the all-you-can-eat breakfast

10. Where was Britain's first seaside pier built?

A. Margate

B. Brighton

C. Ryde

D. Weston Super Mare

11. TRUE or FALSE: The Queen once asked Professor Stephen Hawking why he spoke with an American accent.

12. Which fictional character appeared in a national newspaper poll of 100 great UK citizens?

A. Harry Potter

B. James Bond

C. Mary Poppins

D. Tinky Winky

13. TRUE or FALSE: TV icon Sir David Frost has a memorial in Poets' Corner in Westminster Abbey

14. Who or what can be shot on the Glorious Twelfth?

A. Duck and goose

B. Grey heron and red-breasted mergansers

C. Intruders into the Tower of London

D. Red grouse and ptarmigan

15. Which British film star was denounced as 'a disgusting Jewish acrobat' by the Nazis?

A. Charlie Chaplin

B. Richard Attenborough

C. Trevor Howard

D. Buster Keaton

'There'll always be
an England – even
if it's in Hollywood.'
Bob Hope

16. How did royal grocer Fortnum & Mason get started?

A. By sending a hamper to Buckingham Palace

B. By raising start-up funds through recycling stuff the royals didn't want

C. By offering the Queen a discount on venison

D. By feeding the British Army during the Napoleonic Wars

17. Why was Birmingham schoolmaster Rowland Hill knighted in the mid nineteenth century?

A. He invented the first school examination syllabus

B. He campaigned against corporal punishment in schools

C. He invented the adhesive postage stamp

D. He invented the letter copying machine, the precursor of the Xerox machine

18. Who did Special Branch detective Herbert Fitch spy on in a London pub in 1905?

A. Jack the Ripper

B. Vladimir Lenin

C. Winston Churchill

D. Mata Hari

'[The English] warm their beers and chill their baths and boil all their food, including bread.'

P. J. O'Rourke

19. Which graduates leave university with the highest debt?

A. English

B. Canadian

C. American

D. Australian

20. According to the painter William Hogarth, what was better for you, beer or gin?

A. Gin because it was originally foreign and therefore more exotic

B. Beer because it was English

C. Anything alcoholic would do

D. He was a strict Puritan and hated both

21. What was the name of the BBC's companion soap opera to *EastEnders*?

A. *Little England*

B. *Eldorado*

C. *Brookside*

D. *Walford*

22. What caused Prime Minister Ted Heath a major diplomatic headache with China in 1974?

A. An ultimatum over Hong Kong

B. An unpaid loan

C. Two pandas

D. A shipment of dangerous Christmas tree decorations

23. Which of the following cars is made by a British-owned company?

A. Mini

B. Land Rover

C. Rolls Royce

D. Jaguar

24. Which TWO of the following still live in the wild in the UK?

A. Wolves

B. Wild boar

C. Golden eagle

D. Lynx

Find the answers to this test on p.263.

'Britain, you know; big island off the coast of Europe, rains a lot.'

John O'Farrell

1. Which of the following is NOT illegal?

A. Falling down dead in Parliament

B. Cycling furiously

C. Peeing in a policeman's helmet

D. Sticking a stamp on an envelope with the Queen's head upside down

2. Which of the following has NOT sought devolution from Westminster?

A. Yorkshire

B. Cornwall

C. Liverpool

D. Brighton & Hove

3. Which of the following names from the BBC radio shipping forecast is the odd one out?

A. Forties

B. Dogger

C. Fisher

D. FitzRoy

4. Which of the following postal acronyms used by Second World War soldiers is the least romantic?

A. M.A.L.A.Y.A.

B. N.O.R.W.I.C.H.

C. H.O.L.L.A.N.D.

D. S.W.A.L.K.

5. Common-law couples have the same legal rights as married couples when:

A. They have lived together for more than five years

B. They have lived together for more than two years

C. They have children together

D. None of the above

6. Which of the following celebrities did NOT work as a spy for Britain in the Second World War?

A. Cary Grant

B. Alfred Hitchcock

C. Christopher Lee

D. Greta Garbo

> 'The British do not expect happiness . . . they do not want to be happy. They want to be right.'
>
> *Quentin Crisp*

7. What does the government appointee the Receiver of the Wreck do?

A. Formally receives drunk MPs into the House of Commons sick bay

B. Looks after government vehicles destroyed or damaged in motorway accidents

C. Arranges for the scrappage of military vehicles and ships

D. Deals with abandoned vessels or cargo at sea or washed up on beaches

8. In 1895, the ninth Marquess of Queensberry left a card 'To Oscar Wilde' at his club. What else had he written on it?

A. 'Supposing we discuss this over a sherry?'

B. 'Posing as somdomite [*sic*]'

C. 'Leave my son alone'

D. 'Poseurs and playwrights not welcome'

9. How many Welsh prime ministers have there been?

A. None

B. One

C. Three

D. Seven

10. Which British author earned this opinion on his new manuscript: 'This author is beyond psychiatric help. Do Not Publish!'

A. Will Self

B. Irvine Welsh

C. J. G. Ballard

D. Iain Banks

11. In Shakespeare's time, the average weekly wage was a shilling (12 pence). How much did it cost to attend the theatre?

A. One penny

B. One farthing

C. Sixpence

D. Nothing

12. What was Wallis Simpson supposed to have remarked on hearing her marriage to Edward VII would mean him giving up the crown.

A. 'I have my king. The petty spiteful English can keep their crown.'

B. 'Who cares? We will reign in Spain. Or America. Somewhere with better weather at any rate.'

C. 'The English care nothing about true love.'

D. 'You can't abdicate and eat it.'

13. When Boris Johnson said, 'There are no disasters, only opportunities. And, indeed, opportunities for fresh disasters', what was he referring to?

A. Brexit

B. Black Monday

C. Being sacked over an extramarital affair

D. The failure to fit brakes to 250 'Boris bikes' in London

'It was lovely to talk to the Queen, especially since I am a Windsor too.'

Barbara Windsor

14. Nelson's final signal to the fleet before the Battle of Trafalgar was:

A. 'England expects that every man will do his duty.'

B. 'Engage the enemy more closely.'

C. 'There's a lot more of them than I thought.'

D. 'A case o' rum to he who bags the first Frenchie.'

15. What is the name of the *Desert Island Discs* title music?

A. 'No One Gets Out Of Here Alive'

B. 'The Fatal Shore'

C. 'Splendid Isolation Upon The Shore'

D. 'By The Sleepy Lagoon'

16. Where does the UK rank in the world table of corruption?

A. Least corrupt in world

B. Third least corrupt

C. Fifth least corrupt

D. Tenth least corrupt

17. The Victorians mourned the death of loved ones according to a rigid code. How long was a husband mourned?

A. A year and a day

B. Two years

C. Three years

D. Forty years

18. Which of the following has a criminal record?

A. Princess Anne

B. Theresa May

C. Jeremy Corbyn

D. John Bercow, Speaker of the House of Commons

'In England, people are quite relaxed about a man wearing a dress. But wear the wrong football top in the wrong part of town, you're dead.'

Grayson Perry

19. Why was the OBE known as the Order of the Bad Egg in 1917?

A. Because the Empire had become a source of shame

B. Because you could buy one for £100

C. Because Prime Minister Lloyd George was unpopular

D. Because the King was so unpopular

20. What are the Elgin Marbles?

A. Marbles won by the Earl of Elgin when a pupil at Eton, in a notoriously vicious contest

B. Reproductions of classical Greek sculptures commissioned by the Earl of Elgin

C. Classical marble sculptures taken from Greece by the Earl of Elgin to decorate his house in Scotland

D. Classical marble statues taken from Greece by the Earl of Elgin for the British Museum

21. After arriving in 1948 on the *Empire Windrush*, where did the first Jamaican migrant workers find lodging?

A. Three B&Bs in Brixton

B. Tilbury Fort

C. Harmondsworth detention centre

D. A disused air-raid shelter on Clapham Common

22. In 2011, Barclays chief executive Bob Diamond declared that, for bankers, 'the time for remorse is over'. What happened to him in 2012?

A. He was knighted

B. He was refused a mortgage

C. He resigned

D. He went to jail

23. Who gave the UK's largest-ever charity donation?

A. The Queen

B. Richard Branson

C. Mike Ashley

D. Steve Morgan

24. In June 1940, Winston Churchill made what prediction to his military advisor General Ismay?

A. 'This is not the beginning of the end but the end of the beginning.'

B. 'America will not allow her British cousins to perish against evil.'

C. 'You and I will be dead in three months' time.'

D. 'We will win the Battle of Britain.'

Find the answers to this test on p.269.

Section 2: Test 9

'You never find an Englishman
among the underdogs – except
in England, of course.'

Evelyn Waugh

1. What is the fastest growing type of UK household?

A. Single person

B. Married couple

C. Cohabiting (but unmarried) couple

D. Single parent

2. What was the Rough Wooing?

A. Prince Charles's courtship of Camilla Parker Bowles

B. Premiership footballers' behaviour in nightclubs in the 1970s

C. A war between Scotland and England

D. Violent courtship rites between walruses off the coast of Shetland

3. TRUE or FALSE: There are no female captains in the Royal Navy.

4. What, according to folklore, lies at the bottom of the Chalice Well situated at the foot of Glastonbury Tor?

A. Tent pegs from the very first Glastonbury festival

B. King Arthur's sword

C. Joseph's technicolour dreamcoat

D. The blood of Jesus

5. In the 1970s, Britain came close to war with Iceland in a dispute over:

A. Cod

B. Haddock

C. The right of the Iceland chain to expand on British high streets

D. Immigration

6. TRUE or FALSE: One hundred and seventy British bankers earned bonuses of 1 million euros in 2011.

'They can't stop us eating the British sausage, can they?'

Bernard, Yes, Minister

7. When did the first recorded Chinese restaurant open in the UK and what was it called?

A. Dim Sum Palace, 1807

B. Me Ol' China, 1870

C. The Chinese Restaurant, 1907

D. Wok This Way, 1957

8. Harold Pinter wrote *Betrayal*, a play about his affair with journalist and broadcaster Joan Bakewell, in the 1970s. How did she respond?

A. She sued him

B. She threw a glass of champagne in his face

C. She wrote a play about him

D. She auditioned to be in his play

9. Victorians believed that scientific or literary genius could be sapped by:

A. Too much sleep

B. Socializing with the working class

C. Too much sex

D. Too much small-talk

10. Which ONE of the following phrases was NOT popularized by William Shakespeare?

A. 'Wild goose chase'

B. 'Be all and end all'

C. 'You've got to be cruel to be kind'

D. 'A drop in the bucket'

11. Krishna Bhanji, the first black Briton to win an Oscar, is better known as:

A. Idris Elba

B. Ben Kingsley

C. John Boyega

D. Naomie Harris

12. The front door of 10 Downing Street is made of:

A. Oak from the *Mary Rose*

B. Teak from the desk of Winston Churchill

C. Ash from Captain Cook's ship *Endeavour*

D. Reinforced steel

13. Which TWO coinages do NOT appear in George Orwell's dystopian novel 1984?

A. Groupthink

B. Doublespeak

C. Miniluv

D. Prolefeed

14. Winston Churchill first suggested a united Europe in 1946 and suggested it would be:

A. 'As free and happy as Switzerland is today'

B. 'As free and happy as the United States but with less guns'

C. 'A heady brew of cultures which will prove to many an acquired taste'

D. 'An excellent opportunity for Britons to learn a language'

'If you came from Mars and tried to analyse British or American society through novels, you'd think our society was preponderantly full of middle-aged, slightly alcoholic, middle-class, intellectual men, most of whom are divorced from their families and have nothing to do with children.'

Mark Haddon

15. If you find valuable old coins, how old must they be in order to be declared 'treasure'?

A. 100 years old

B. 200 years old

C. 300 years old

D. It is their gold or silver content, not their age, which is important

16. Which ONE of the following was NOT an offence abolished by the Criminal Law Act of 1967?

A. Challenging someone to fight

B. Eavesdropping

C. Being a common scold (e.g. berating neighbours)

D. Flatulence in the street

17. Why is there a pronounced bend on the London Underground's Piccadilly Line between South Kensington and Knightsbridge?

A. To avoid the Queen's underground bullion store

B. To avoid a mass grave for plague victims

C. To avoid an underground nuclear missile silo, London's main defence against nuclear attack

D. To avoid dense igneous rock which made tunnelling prohibitively expensive

18. **Britannia, pictured on coins with shield and spear, had a daughter. What was her name?**

A. Brittany

B. Little Britain

C. Zealandia

D. Little England

'The English contribution to world cuisine – the chip.'

John Cleese

19. **In the eighteenth century, John Bull became popular as a symbolic stout, plain-speaking Brit. What was the name of his French adversary?**

A. Francois Frog

B. Jean Claude Calamity

C. Marcel Moron

D. Louis Baboon

20. **In the Middle Ages, having no means of support or being a 'vagabond' entitled you to:**

A. Three nights' food and lodging in a hostelry

B. Three nights in the stocks

C. An apprenticeship with a carpenter or other trade

D. Twenty lashes

21. TRUE or FALSE: Under UK law, a mother can conceal her true identity from her own children under exceptional circumstances

22. The following are all obsolete Victorian jobs. Which one was a trader of dog faeces?

A. A mudlark

B. A tosher

C. A pure finder

D. A chaunter

23. Who gave the acclaimed 'The Three Dimensions of a Complete Life' sermon in St Paul's Cathedral?

A. Thomas Cranmer

B. Cardinal Wolsey

C. The Dalai Lama

D. Martin Luther King Jr

24. What proportion of the UK population are Muslim?

A. 21 per cent

B. 5 per cent

C. 32 per cent

D. 10 per cent

Find the answers to this test on p.274.

Section 2: Test 10

'Britain has had the same foreign policy objective for at least the last 500 years: to create a disunited Europe . . . Now that we're inside we can make a complete pig's breakfast of the whole thing.'

Sir Humphrey Appleby, Yes, Minister

1. The Met Office predicts a two-degree Celsius rise in the UK's south-west over the next 40 years. As a result:

A. There will be more shark attacks off the Cornish coast

B. There will be widespread drought and soil erosion

C. The area will become suitable for citrus cultivation

D. Cornwall will replace the Riviera for the Eurotrash jet set

2. A cross-party committee of MPs declared a UK public health emergency in 2016. Why?

A. Obesity statistics showed British children were fatter than ever

B. Alcohol consumption reached dangerous proportions

C. Cancer survival rates were declared the worst in Europe

D. Pollution was declared to be killing thousands

3. Which of the following countries is the most densely populated?

A. China

B. Nigeria

C. Pakistan

D. The UK

4. Operation Chastise was the official name for:

A. The police hunt for the Yorkshire Ripper in the 1970s

B. The Dambusters raid on Germany in 1943

C. The police hunt for the Brink's-Mat gold bullion robbers in the 1980s

D. The special forces operation to extradite Julian Assange

5. Which was the first ever BBC TV outside broadcast?

A. The 1937 coronation of George VI

B. The coronation of Elizabeth II in 1953

C. The Grand National horse race at Aintree in 1962

D. The FA Cup final at Wembley in 1964

6. The words 'blag', 'naff' and 'clobber' are all examples of what?

A. Cockney rhyming slang

B. Jamaican patois

C. London theatre slang

D. Royal Navy slang

Q

'The English feel *Schadenfreude* even about themselves.'

Martin Amis

7. What did the Queen give Paul Burrell, butler of Diana, Princess of Wales, after Diana's death?

A. A Versace gown embroidered with pearls

B. A thick ear

C. A dire warning

D. A cottage on her Sandringham estate

8. Royal Navy officers make a series of after-dinner toasts which differ each day. What do they toast on Thursdays?

A. 'Our ships at sea'

B. 'A bloody war or a sickly season'

C. 'A willing foe and sea room'

D. 'Pirates wielding a blunt cutlass'

9. TRUE or FALSE: The inscription on Nelson's tomb in St Paul's Cathedral misspells his name

10. In 2017, the great-grandson of polar explorer Sir Ernest Shackleton reached the South Pole travelling in:

A. His great-grandfather's sledge

B. A microlight aircraft

C. A Hyundai Santa Fe

D. A Toyota Yaris

11. Why did James Kirkup's poem 'The Love That Dares to Speak Its Name' achieve notoriety in 1976?

A. It won the first Bad Sex Award

B. It was the subject of the last successful blasphemy trial

C. It was written by Princess Margaret's chauffeur, dedicated to her and published in the *News of the World*

D. It openly celebrated paedophilia, and the author was jailed

12. In the darkest days of the Second World War, Winston Churchill seriously considered:

A. A negotiated peace with Hitler

B. Britain and France uniting as one country

C. Britain and America uniting as one country

D. Britain attacking Russia

13. Which of the following have turned down an official honour (e.g. OBE, CBE or knighthood) from the Queen?

A. John Lennon

B. French & Saunders

C. Professor Stephen Hawking

D. David Bowie

14. Why are there stone pineapples on the western towers of St Paul's Cathedral?

A. They were architect Sir Christopher Wren's favourite fruit

B. The towers were sponsored by a consortium of wealthy merchants trading with the West Indies

C. Pineapples symbolized peace, prosperity and status

D. Stonemasons had originally carved human heads. Wren thought them too gruesome and the cheapest option was to change them into pineapples

'The way to endure summer in England is to have it framed and glazed in a comfortable room.'

Horace Walpole

15. What caused the Great Storm of 1987?

A. Michael Fish

B. A hurricane

C. Global warming

D. A sting jet

16. A 2015 Bank of England report estimated half of all banknotes are used for what?

A. Snorting cocaine

B. Birthday gifts to children

C. Gambling

D. Drug dealing, prostitution, fraud, human trafficking and tax avoidance

17. Which guest on BBC Radio 4's *Desert Island Discs* chose exclusively their own recordings?

A. Elizabeth Schwarzkopf

B. Norman Wisdom

C. Dame Moura Lympany

D. Rolf Harris

18. What can you find on 92 per cent of baby-changing facilities installed in the north-west?

A. Traces of poo

B. Traces of vomit

C. Traces of cocaine

D. Graffiti

19. In Victorian Britain, what service did a costermonger provide?

A. He was an accountant

B. He sold fruit and vegetables

C. He helped with travellers' luggage on stage coaches

D. He was a shoe-shiner

20. Which of the following are banned under the 1991 Dangerous Dogs Act?

A. Staffordshire Bull Terrier

B. Japanese Tosa

C. Dogo Argentino

D. Fila Brasiliero

21. Which of the following did Aldous Huxley predict in his 1932 novel *Brave New World*?

A. A powerful elite controlling the world through the media

B. Sedation of unruly children with pharmaceuticals

C. A national lottery

D. Corruption in elite sport

22. Where does Britain rank globally in military spending?

A. Third

B. Tenth

C. Fifteenth

D. Fifth

23. In 2010, actor Helen Mirren complained about Hollywood's treatment of which social group?

A. Women over 30

B. Actors of colour

C. Plus-size women

D. Well-spoken people with a British accent

> **'All Englishmen talk as if they've got a bushel of plums stuck in their throats, and then after swallowing them get constipated from the pits.'**
>
> *W. C. Fields*

24. The richest 1 per cent of UK earners pay what proportion of UK income tax?

A. 27.5 per cent

B. 20 per cent

C. 9 per cent

D. 15 per cent

Find the answers to this test on p.279.

Section 2: Test 11

> **'The English certainly and fiercely pride themselves in never praising themselves.'**
>
> *Wyndham Lewis*

1. TRUE or FALSE: Angela Smith is the leader of the opposition.

2. What is meant by the 'demise of the Crown'?

A. The decline in respect for the Royal Family dating from their appearance in *It's a Royal Knockout* in 1987

B. The decline of royal power dating from the execution of Charles I

C. The end of any royal reign by death or abdication

D. A play by Christopher Marlowe which was deemed treasonous

3. What was the Anglo-Saxon goddess Frigg's chief realm of influence?

A. Blasphemy

B. Fridays

C. Love

D. Chastity

4. 'God Save The Queen' is the national anthem of:

A. England

B. New Zealand

C. Great Britain

D. None of the above

5. Adultery, in the eyes of British law, is:

A. Grounds for divorce

B. No longer grounds for divorce

C. No longer adultery in the eyes of the law if you have separated from your spouse

D. Punishable by stoning

Bishop to waitress: 'Young lady, I would rather commit adultery than take an intoxicating beverage.' Churchill to waitress: 'Come back, lassie, I didn't know we had a choice!'

Apocryphal story about *Winston Churchill*

6. Which TWO of the following are slang for an Army disciplinary meeting?

A. An interview without coffee

B. A carpet parade

C. A meeting with tea and no biscuits

D. A little walk in the woods

7. Which of the following is against the law?

A. To sit in a bus seat marked out for the infirm, the pregnant or the elderly

B. To jump the queue in the London Underground ticket hall

C. To pull strings with the bouncer to enter a club

D. To cross the road when a fire engine passes by

8. In 1778, John Stafford Smith wrote a boozy hymn to wine called 'To Anacreon In Heaven'. It is now known as:

A. 'Knees Up Mother Brown'

B. 'All For Me Grog'

C. 'The Star Spangled Banner'

D. 'Swing Low Sweet Chariot'

9. Immigrants constitute what proportion of the population of the UK?

A. 11 per cent

B. 25 per cent

C. 6 per cent

D. 13 per cent

> **'Britain, Britain, Britain. Everybody is welcome in Britain. We are open 'til six, Monday to Saturday. No foreign gentlemen, please.'**
>
> Narrator, *Little Britain*

10. TRUE or FALSE: During the Second World War, the British planned to use chemical weapons on the Germans.

11. What is the Privy Council?

A. The council responsible for the upkeep of Buckingham Palace and its grounds

B. The team of royal attendants who accompany the monarch and arrange toilet facilities for her when she is out and about

C. The monarch's panel of advisers drawn from senior politicians and civil servants, as well as other royals

D. The local council department presiding over public lavatories

12. Who was Mondeo Man?

A. He was Greenpeace's all-British superhero, created to rival Superman and save the earth

B. He was the prime suspect in a series of unsolved murders in the 1990s

C. He inspired Tony Blair to form New Labour

D. He was a robot invented to promote the Ford motor company's popular saloon model

13. Which British construction project has been variously credited to a wizard, aliens and the Romans?

A. The Shard

B. Castlerigg Stone Circle

C. Stonehenge

D. Silbury Hill

14. What was a 'molly house' in eighteenth- and nineteenth-century Britain?

A. A gay hang-out

B. A women's refuge

C. An opium den

D. A home for infant orphans

15. TRUE or FALSE: The UK is almost £1 trillion in debt.

16. Which British rock star once got into trouble with the US authorities?

A. Sid Vicious

B. John Lennon

C. Ozzy Osbourne

D. Liam Gallagher

17. Why did Tory prime minister Anthony Eden consider taking control of the BBC in 1956?

A. To schedule more costume dramas

B. To prepare for privatizing the Corporation

C. To make it support a war

D. To censor excessive sex and violence

18. TRUE or FALSE: Mrs Thatcher considered plans for a suspension bridge to link Britain and France

19. During the Cold War, where did the UK government plan to operate from in the event of a major nuclear strike?

A. Stornoway in the Outer Hebrides

B. Edinburgh

C. Wiltshire

D. Isle of Wight

'In left-wing circles, it is always felt that there is something slightly disgraceful in being an Englishman, and that it is a duty to snigger at every English institution, from horse racing to suet puddings.'

George Orwell

20. What do former Australian prime minister Paul Keating, US basketball star LeBron James and Michelle Obama have in common?

A. They have all served time in jail

B. They are all related to Jeremy Corbyn

C. They have all caused a royal scandal

D. They all hold British passports

21. TRUE or FALSE: The UK has the fastest average internet speed in the world.

22. Which of the following countries has the most UNESCO Cultural World Heritage Sites?

A. Italy

B. China

C. France

D. UK

23. Who was the winner of 'the worst Briton' of all time in a 2002 Channel 4 poll?

A. Tony Blair

B. Jack the Ripper

C. Oswald Mosley

D. Jordan

24. What did construction workers digging beneath London's O2 Arena (formerly the Millennium Dome) unearth in 2017?

A. The skeleton of Viking King Sweyn Forkbeard

B. A tunnel labelled 'Evacuation route for Peter Mandelson, John Prescott and Tony Blair'

C. A Teletubby

D. A plague pit

25. Bonus question: Which of the following is a British expression of excellence?

A. The cat's pyjamas

B. The bee's knees

C. The dog's bollocks

D. The dog's breakfast

Find the answers to this test on p.284.

ANSWERS
Section 1: UK Citizenship Level

1. C: The United Kingdom of Great Britain and Northern Ireland

It's the whole mouthful. However, the country may soon have to be renamed 'the United Kingdom of Great Britain not including Scotland, holding on to Wales's hand very tightly and increasingly nervous about Northern Ireland'.

2. B: Civil service pension

Civil servants do not have to rely on their NI contributions for their generous government pensions. According to the 2016 accounts of main Whitehall departments, 42 senior civil servants retired with pension funds of over £1 million.

3. TRUE

Julius Caesar came, saw, but did not conquer. The successful Roman invasion occurred later, in AD 43, under Emperor Claudius.

4. C: South-east Europe

According to *Life in the UK*, the first farmers 'probably' came from south-east Europe. But in spite of this vagueness, this is still a 'fact' they do feel you must know. (NB: there were no European farm subsidies during the Neolithic Age.)

5. C: All women over 30 who were householders . . .

The legislation enfranchised almost 8.5 million women, 43 per cent of the electorate. Viscount Helmsley, speaking in opposition to the Conciliation Bill of 1912, typified the argument against women's suffrage thus: 'The way in which certain types of women, easily recognised, have acted in the last year or two, especially in the last few weeks, lends a great deal of colour to the argument that the mental equilibrium of the female sex is not as stable as the mental equilibrium of the male sex.'

6. B: A magistrate need have no legal qualifications and works for nothing

This may explain why the magistrates' bench so often resembles a golf club AGM or a meeting at the Women's Institute.

7. C: Make a small claim online

Small claims are now dealt with online. 'I don't want money. It is only people who pay their bills who want money and I never pay mine' – Oscar Wilde.

8. B: Irish Gaelic

'If there were only three Irishmen left in the world you'd find two of them in a corner talking about the other' – Brendan Behan.

9. D: Traffic lights

They were invented by an American, Lester Wire, in 1914.

10. A: 'God save your mad parade'

This is from 'God Save The Queen' by the Sex Pistols.

11. B: It has no name.

Britain has an unwritten constitution based on a set of unwritten laws, principles and conventions. In *Life in the UK,* it is explained that 'an unwritten constitution allows for more flexibility and better government'. i.e. it makes it possible to make it up as you go along.

12. D: Festival of Lights

No, that crazy festival you're thinking of when you assault each other with coloured powder is called Holi.

13. D: The Nobel Prize in Literature

Kipling was awarded the Literature Nobel aged 42 and remains the youngest ever winner, one of a total of eight British Literature laureates (compared to France's 17). In spite of Britain's dominant world position in literature, the majority of Britain's 117 Nobel Prize wins have been for chemistry and physiology or medicine.

14. B: 10 per cent

Life in the UK states: 'Post-war immigration means that nearly 10 per cent of the population has a parent or grandparent born outside the UK. The UK continues to be a multinational and multiracial society with a rich and varied culture.'

15. C: John Masefield

He was a poet. But some may be surprised to see David Allan, an eighteenth-century Scottish portrait painter, and John Petts, a Welsh engraver and stained-glass artist, listed in *Life in the UK* alongside more famous names like John Constable, Henry Moore and David Hockney as British artists all prospective citizens should know about.

16. C: The Queen

UK laws are made in the name of the Crown as Sovereign, which means the Queen is effectively above the law. At the 2007 inquest into the death of Diana, Princess of Wales, Michael Mansfield QC raised the possibility that Her Majesty would be asked to give evidence in her own court. The coroner ruled it would not further the inquest process.

17. A: Nominate life peers

Peerages are supposed to reward great public service. However, the 2006 'Cash for Honours' scandal suggested it was more about the recipients' ability to offer substantial loans. The Labour government was investigated by the police, but no charges were brought.

18. FALSE

Between 1801 and 1901 the UK population grew 500 per cent, from 8 million to 40 million. Between 1901 to 2005 it grew only 50 per cent, from 40 million to just under 60 million.

19. A and C: Weapons training and passing a citizenship test

These are not on the curriculum of the National Citizen Service, which is aimed at 15 to 17 year olds, to help them develop life skills and boost their CVs. Although how experience of picking up litter will impress future employers is hard to grasp.

20. D: The Bronze Age

The ancient British art of brass rubbing was not yet invented.

21. A: Ireland united with England, Wales and Scotland to form the United Kingdom

The Acts of Union marked the official bringing together of Ireland with the other nations to form the United Kingdom. The countries had previously been joined in 'personal union' by Henry VIII, but now the bond became legal, fiscal and parliamentary. And then, of course, they all lived happily ever after.

22. A: An employer to ask her to leave her job

For many employers, a woman's place was still barefoot, pregnant and in the kitchen.

23. A and C: He designed the Cenotaph and New Delhi

Lutyens did also design Queen Mary's dolls' house, now on permanent display at Windsor Castle.

24. FALSE

You can donate a kidney while living. However, you must be dead before you donate your heart.

TEST 1

UK Citizenship Level: ANSWERS

1. D: A prehistoric village

Skara Brae in Orkney is the best preserved prehistoric village in northern Europe. Inhabited 5,000 years ago, the settlement has nine almost identical houses with storage boxes on the floors and storage spaces in the walls. Discovery of a Neolithic Ikea nearby cannot be far off.

2. D: Because he often said a place 'had capabilities'

This 'capabilities' quote is the somewhat vague explanation *Life in the UK* gives for Brown's name. Presumably these days he'd just be called Lancelot 'Decking' Brown and be done with it.

3. B: The Gambia

A major destination for female sex tourists and with a dictator, Yahya Jammeh, who believed he had a herbal cure for AIDS, Gambia left the Commonwealth because it was considered 'neo-colonial'. However, Boris Johnson recently revealed that with Jammeh now in exile, there are plans afoot for its return.

4. B: Slaves to be freed and slavery made illegal

This was the end of slavery in Britain. But Ceylon (Sri Lanka) and St Helena were exempt from the emancipation of slaves, at the insistence of the East India Company. Still, at least in this we Brits beat the Americans by 32 years, and they had to fight a civil war about it first.

5. C: Mary Peters

She won with a world-record points tally. Lancashire-born but a Northern Ireland resident, Peters received death threats on returning home to Belfast because she was a Protestant.

6. C: Upholds human rights among EU member states

It was the Council of Europe which first drafted the European Convention on Human Rights. And it was Winston Churchill who, in 1946, first called for 'a kind of United States of Europe' and for the formation of the Council of Europe.

7. D: 1969

The voting age was reduced to 18 in 1969. A further reduction to 16 was considered in 1999 but defeated in the Commons by 434 to 36 votes. In Scotland, the voting age for Scottish and local government elections was reduced to 16 by a bill passed in the Scottish Parliament in 2015.

8. C: A novelist of any gender from the Commonwealth, Ireland or Zimbabwe

But *Life in the UK* states in a marginal note: 'Since 2014 the Man Booker Prize is awarded for fiction novels originally written in English and published in the UK by authors from anywhere in the world. However, for the purposes of your test you must learn the material as reproduced here.' I.e. you must give the wrong answer to pass the test.

9. FALSE

England welcomed immigrants. French weavers, German engineers, Italian glass-blowers and Dutch canal builders all made contributions to enrich English life, according to *Life in the UK*.

10. B: The law applied according to precedence and tradition

English common law is the most widely used legal system in the world, with an estimated 30 per cent of the world population living under it or something similar. Yet because it isn't actually written down, it is open to much general misinterpretation, such as the idea that there are any legal rights attached to a 'common-law marriage'.

11. FALSE

Women had to wait until the passage of the Matrimonial Causes Act of 1857, the success of which was partly due to the intense campaigning of Caroline Norton, granddaughter of the playwright Richard Sheridan, who struggled for over 20 years to escape from her violent husband, a Tory MP.

12. B: The Duke of Wellington

The victor of the Battle of Waterloo, whom Tennyson hailed as 'the last great Englishman'.

13. B: 'Anthem for Doomed Youth' by Wilfred Owen

Prospective UK citizens (and UK schoolkids) must still learn First World War poetry. However, during a debate to mark the 2014 centenary of the opening hostilities of the Great War, Jeremy Paxman noted: 'All that is taught is about the pointless sacrifice. It's not helpful to see the whole thing through the eyes of poetry . . . Luxuriating in the horror of the thing really won't do and doesn't set out to answer really interesting questions.'

14. A and B: Protect a person from being forced into a marriage, and protect a person already in a forced marriage

Anyone breaching an FMPO can be sent to jail for two years.

15. B: Celtic

English developed later. And as Norman St John-Stevas once said: 'How amazing that the language of a few thousand savages living on a fog-encrusted island in the North Sea should become the language of the world.'

16. D: 870 miles

But neither of these landmarks represents the true extremities of Britain's landmass. Dunnet Head in Caithness is the most northerly point, while Lizard Point takes the title in the south.

17. D: The ability to laugh at ourselves

The book also recommends the traditions of comedy and satire as embodied in venerable magazines like *Punch* (final issue 2002) and *Private Eye*.

18. TRUE

Though overruling the Lords is a prerogative rarely used. The 2004 Hunting Act was the last time the so-called Parliament Act was invoked by the Commons to overrule the Lords. Despite the Burns Report of 2000 concluding that fox hunting 'seriously compromises the welfare of the fox', the Lords would not agree on the terms of a ban. The Commons pushed a ban through, but not before anti-hunt protestors stormed the Commons chamber, the first unauthorized invasion since 1641.

19. D: First past the post

This means the candidate with the most votes in any one constituency wins the seat, regardless of the overall vote for their party in the country as a whole. The Electoral Reform Society opposes the first-past-the-post system since it concentrates power in an unrepresentative fashion. For example, in Scotland in 2015, the SNP won just under half the votes but won 95 per cent of the seats.

20. A: Music halls

Like many comedians of their generation, Morecambe and Wise started in music halls. **Ernie:** 'Don't say that – you make us sound like a cheap music-hall act'. **Eric:** 'But we *are* a cheap music-hall act. (The boy's a fool.)'

21. A: The Union flag

It is often stated that the term Union Jack should only be used when the flag flies from the jack mast (the short mast at the bow) of a ship, though this is also disputed.

22. C: Rudyard Kipling

Baden Powell's cub scout movement were so inspired by Kipling's fictional wolf Akela that they adopted him as their leader. Hence the cub scout vow: 'Akela, we will do our best!'

23. C: Free secondary education for all children in England and Wales

In 1938, around 80 per cent of children left school at fourteen, and fewer than one in a hundred made it to university. Tory MP Rab Butler's Act made provision for free secondary education for all, in a mixture of grammar, technical and secondary-modern schools.

24. C: The monarch's heirs and successors

This seems to stretch loyalty unreasonably far. Must we also be loyal to all they say and do? What about, say, the Prince of Wales's Duchy of Cornwall pork sausages?

Section 1: Test 3

1. C: The right to justice for every man regardless of social status

As *1066 and All That** so memorably put it: 'no one was to be put to death, save for some reason (except the Common People)', and 'the Barons should not be tried except by a jury of other Barons who would understand'.

2. D: AMs (Assembly Members)

There are 60 Assembly Members in total, 40 covering constituencies and 20 covering regions, if you really want to know.

3. A: Albania

Britain is still a member at the time of writing!

4. D: Scotland

Northern Ireland is separate, as the official name of the country is the United Kingdom of Great Britain and Northern Ireland. The Isle of Man is a Crown Dependency, while St Helena is an overseas territory; both are linked with, but not part of, Great Britain.

5. C: James VII

What seems most significant about this king is not his number but that he was a Catholic, often seen as a threat to the Crown in British history.

6. D: A gift

Gifts are tax free, but there can be a hitch down the line, involving inheritance tax.

---

*A tongue-in-cheek schoolboy history of Britain by W. C. Sellar and R. J. Yeatman first published in 1930; it has curious echoes in the history put forward in the *Life in the UK* handbook.

T
E
S
T

3

UK Citizenship Level: ANSWERS

7. C: Wales

The Union Jack consists of the crosses of St George (England), St Andrew (Scotland) and St Patrick (Northern Ireland). The Welsh dragon was left off because Wales was already united with England when the first Union flag was created in 1606 from the flags of England and Scotland. Ask any Welshman what he thinks of that excuse.

8. C: Games can last for five days and still end in a draw

Life in the UK says: 'the idiosyncratic nature of the game and its complex laws are said to reflect the best of the British character and sense of fair play'. It symbolizes qualities that other nations have been eager to emulate, for example President Robert Mugabe of Zimbabwe: 'Cricket civilizes people and creates good gentlemen. I want everyone to play cricket in Zimbabwe. I want ours to be a nation of gentlemen.'

9. D: He was the king who united Scotland against the Vikings

Kenneth the First, the unlikely sounding first King of Scotland, is an ancestor of our current Queen Elizabeth II.

10. B: He was a ship's surgeon on a whaling ship

While still a medical student, Conan Doyle worked as a doctor on SS *Hope*, a Greenland whaling ship. But he spent more time preventing fights between crew members than practising medicine. Later, he commented: 'I came of age at 80 degrees north latitude.'

11. C: Barrows

Though why knowing this would qualify you to become a British citizen (unless you had a particular interest in archaeology) is unclear

12. D: A Norman castle keep

However, *Life in the UK* does not make clear what a 'keep' is or why it is important.

13. B and C: They broke windows and committed arson, and they went on hunger strike

'The argument of the broken window pane is the most valuable argument in modern politics' – Emmeline Pankhurst

14. C: India

Estimates of the number of Indian troops killed in the Great War vary between 40,00 and over 70,000.

15. A: 23 April

Curiously, St George shares a birthday with that great Englishman William Shakespeare. It has also been designated as World Book Day.

16. D: 59 per cent

In the 2011 Census, 59 per cent of people identified themselves as Christian (not necessarily practising). Only 4.8 per cent identified as Muslim, 1.5 per cent as Hindu, 0.8 per cent as Sikh and 0.5 per cent each as Jewish or Buddhist. Meanwhile, 0.3 per cent claimed to be Jedi Knights, so we may be leaving Europe but hopefully the Force will be with us!

17. B: At least every five years

Under the 2011 Fixed-terms Parliament Act, an election must be called at least every five years. But D is also correct, in that the prime minister may call one at any time before that, as seen in 2017's snap election.

18. B: The Episcopal Church

It is also known under this name in America but as the Anglican church in other countries. The Church of England has existed since the Reformation and was exported to the American colonies, and then all over the world under the British Empire.

19. B: An area around Dublin ruled by the English in the Middle Ages

The word derives from the Latin for 'stake' or fence-post, as the territory was once fortified. The term is still in common usage to describe Dublin and its suburbs.

20. C: Russian and Polish Jews

Russian Jews in particular came to escape anti-Semitic laws and the pogroms. Today, Britain, which was spared the effects of the Nazi holocaust, has the largest Jewish population in Europe after France.

21. C: Citizens in British colonies of North America

'Taxation without representation is tyranny!' became a slogan for the rebellious colonists during the American War of Independence.

22. B: The Pope would not give permission for his divorce

All that upheaval in order to acquire a younger wife. These days he'd just go on Tinder.

23. B: In a hotel or restaurant when eating with someone aged 18 or over

After the age of 16, drinking with a meal out is permitted if accompanied by an adult. You couldn't get away with it in the US, where the underage drinking laws are a lot stricter. But giving kids over the age of five diluted wine to drink is quite normal in France.

24. A: The Commonwealth

The Monarchists refused to use the name, preferring to call it 'the Interregnum'. That seventeenth-century Commonwealth is in no way related to the institution that today consists of most of the countries that were formerly part of the British Empire.

1. B: The Scottish court for young offenders

The system is run by 3,000 volunteers across Scotland who give up an afternoon every two weeks to hear children's cases.

2. D: The licensee

The Licensing Act 2003 gives large discretion to pub and nightclub owners and was intended to stem the culture of 'binge-drinking'. A government report subsequently admitted that the results provided 'a mixed picture'.

3. B: Pocket boroughs

These were almost as bad as rotten boroughs, where the constituency was so small that the seat could effectively be bought. In 1802, Sir William Paxton bought his Carmarthenshire seat with 11,070 breakfasts, 36,901 dinners and 25,275 gallons of ale.

4. C: The ATM (or cashpoint)

The Home Office's book also requires you to know it first came into use in 1967 at the Barclays branch in Enfield, north London.

5. A: A German refugee living in Buckinghamshire

Dr Sir Ludwig Guttmann was treating patients with spinal injuries at Stoke Mandeville Hospital in the 1940s and recommended that they undertake physical exercise. Unable to resist competing with each other, their rehabilitation sessions grew into the Paralympics.

6. C: Ofcom

Ofcom is the independent regulator and competition authority for communications organizations like the BBC. The other organizations all work to influence parliamentary decision-makers.

7. FALSE

Each country has its own civil service.

8. C: Pioneering steam-powered textile machinery

Life in the UK tells us that when the bottom fell out of the wigs market, Arkwright turned to textiles and introduced a new form of carding machine as well as horse-driven spinning mills. Later, he used the steam engine to power his machines.

9. A: The hills

Of course, the more famous part of the quote is 'We shall fight on the beaches'. Interestingly, in the same speech Churchill predicted that if Britain were invaded: 'our Empire beyond the seas, armed and guarded by the British Fleet, would carry on the struggle, until, in God's good time, the New World, with all its power and might, steps forth to the rescue and the liberation of the old'.

10. C: A widespread famine

Potato blight caused the Great Hunger of 1845 and triggered the greatest mass migration of the nineteenth century. Charles Trevelyan was the British government's civil servant in charge of famine relief efforts and he was clearly no Bob Geldof. He noted: 'The judgement of God sent the calamity to teach the Irish a lesson, that calamity must not be too much mitigated.' In seven years, one million Irish died and the country's population was halved.

11. D: To protect and fight for your country

Life in the UK gives a long list of the 'values and responsibilities' expected of a British citizen, which, as well as A, B and C above, also includes: 'to work to provide for yourself and your family' and 'to treat everyone equally, regardless of sex, race, religion, age, disability, class or sexual orientation'.

12. D: With a battle at Bosworth Field

During the battle, Richard III of the House of York was killed. Or, according to the delightful muddle of Sellar and Yeatman, he tried to give his kingdom to a horse. In any case, this ended the Plantagenet dynasty and made way for the Tudor line.

13. D: Somalia

Sir Mohamed Farah moved to Britain as a child and was naturalized as a British citizen when he was 15. His early ambition was to become a car mechanic or an Arsenal right winger. He is the most decorated British athlete of all time.

14. FALSE

Only the Scottish Parliament has the power to legislate on matters of civil and criminal law. The Welsh government can only legislate in agreed devolved areas like agriculture, education and town planning.

15. C: Gothic Revival

Augustus Pugin, architect of the nineteenth-century redesign of the Palace of Westminster, believed that reviving the medieval gothic style was the most authentic expression of English identity. St Pancras is his fellow Victorian architect Gilbert Scott's masterpiece and was used as a location for Hogwarts in the *Harry Potter* films.

16. A: To defend the Roman Empire under attack elsewhere

Roman occupation ended because Emperor Honorius needed help fighting off the German Visigoths who were attacking Rome. Germans helping Britain gain freedom from invasion? We never really said thanks, did we?

17. A: The monarch must be born British.

Just as well, because William of Orange had just come over from Holland with his wife Mary and there would be a German (George I) on the throne within 50 years.

18. B: Oliver Cromwell

Cromwell's lofty title was rather different in tone to the new constitution, which was known as the 'Humble Petition and Advice'.

19. TRUE

However, the Northern Ireland Parliament was abolished again at the start of the Troubles in 1972. The Northern Ireland Assembly was then established in 1998 following the Good Friday Agreement.

20. D: Everyone

By law, a local authority must make the electoral register available for all to see upon request. Why don't you pop down with a picnic and make a day of it?

21. A: He is always optimistic.

But Mr Micawber also famously said: 'Annual income twenty pounds, annual expenditure nineteen pounds nineteen and six, result happiness. Annual income twenty pounds, annual expenditure twenty pounds ought and six, result misery.' Most Chancellors of the Exchequer could have learned a lesson from that.

22. FALSE

The Angles and Saxons failed to conquer the west of England, as well as much of Wales and Scotland.

23. B: It absorbed some Norman French influences and became the official language.

The 100,000 Norman French words added to English included parliament, government, boot and roast. Regarding the last, ironically, a thousand years later the French threw '*rosbif*' back at us as an insult.

24. B: The Welsh Assembly building

The Senedd is heated by geothermal energy, and its toilets are flushed by rainwater from the roof. Not sure about the heating, but anyone who's been to Wales will know the toilets probably flush really well.

1. C: The Norman Conquest of 1066

As Sellar and Yeatman pointed out in *1066 and All That*: 'The Norman Conquest was a Good Thing, as from this time onwards England stopped being conquered and thus was able to become top nation.'

2. C: Public sewers were introduced in London

A concerted effort to create a sewerage system had to wait for the Great Stink of 1858.

3. A: Three: Lords, Commons and Clergy

They were called Estates, although only the Lords (Lairds) were lucky enough to control vast swathes of the Highlands.

4. B: Britain against France and Spain

The French and Spanish navies had 33 ships, Nelson's Royal Navy had 27. The English fleet won by 22 ships to 0.

5. C: Robert Browning

It is from Browning's 'Home-Thoughts, from Abroad', a poem that of course all British citizens can recite by heart.

6. D: John Macleod

Although insulin is acclaimed in *Life in the UK* as a great British invention, the book omits to mention that the Scottish physician John Macleod's co-discoverers were three Canadian scientists.

7. C: Sir Carol Reed (also a man, in spite of the name)

In *Life in the UK*, the highly selective list of famous British films you should be familiar with goes right up to date with 2003's *Touching the Void*, directed by Kevin Macdonald.

8. C and D: Allegiance to the Crown, and pride in British culture

Only 16 of the 52 Commonwealth countries currently recognize Elizabeth II as queen. But she is also Paramount Chief of Fiji.

9. A and C: Shoddy work by a builder and excessive bank charges

Civil law derives from Roman law and relates to the individual and the community. Yes, smoking in a prohibited area is a criminal offence, as is being drunk on an aircraft.

10. B: On foot

There was still a land bridge connecting Britain with mainland Europe at that time.

11. C: A person is renting a room and has a separate tenancy agreement

So those 25 Albanian fruit pickers living in separate bedsits round the corner? They should each have a licence if they want to watch *EastEnders*.

12. B: Attend the House of Lords

Hereditary peers no longer have an automatic right to attend the House of Lords but can elect a few of their number as their representatives.

13. B: 'Auld Lang Syne'

Burns heard the traditional folk song and had the music formally transcribed and set to his own words.

14. A: Steel

The Bessemer process for making steel gave rise to British shipbuilding and railways.

15. D: Aneurin Bevan

He was the Minister for Health in Clement Attlee's government, and the NHS grew out of the Beveridge Report, which promised to introduce the welfare state. Bev Bevan, no relation, was the drummer in the Electric Light Orchestra.

16. B: The area of Britain settled by the Vikings

They settled mainly in the north and east, where many place names, like Grimsby and Scunthorpe, and places ending with 'howe' (village) or 'thorp' (hamlet) are derived from the Viking language.

17. A: 1928

After women over 30 had been granted the vote in 1918, the Representation of the People Act 1928 gave all women aged 21 or over the vote. In the following year's election, it meant 5 million more women were suddenly eligible to vote – over half the electorate. Not that everyone was happy about it. Irish poet John Boyle O'Reilly claimed: 'Woman suffrage is an unjust, unreasonable, unspiritual abnormality. It is a hard, undigested, tasteless, devitalized proposition. It is a half-fledged, unmusical, Promethean abomination. It is a quack bolus to reduce masculinity even by the obliteration of femininity.'

18. C: Eight

The authors of *Life in the UK* acknowledge that in actual fact there are *nine* candles but insist that, for the purposes of the test, you must give the answer eight.

19. B: New Year

Known of course as Hogmanay – 'Lang may yer lum reek!'

20. A: 18

The youngest person elected to Parliament since 1667 is Mhairi Black (SNP), who was 20 years old when she was elected in 2015. She retained her seat in the 2017 election.

T E S T 5

UK Citizenship Level: ANSWERS

21. D: Polo

Polo originated in Asia. The search goes on for a sport we British can both invent and be good at.

22. B: Three anonymous volunteers

Its stated mission is: 'to promote the preservation of places of historic interest and natural beauty . . . for the benefit of the nation'.

23. B: Welsh music, dance and poetry is performed.

Local festivities date back 800 years, but the national celebration of Welsh culture became popular after an 1847 government report into local education concluded the Welsh were 'ignorant, lazy and immoral'.

24. C: Ayr

Ayr Racecourse is 37 miles south of Glasgow. Red Rum was the first and only horse to win both the Scottish and the English Grand National in the same year, 1974.

Section 1: Test 6

1. C: Loch Lomond (71 km²)

Lough Neagh in Northern Ireland is over five times its size at 383 km², but *Life in the UK* overlooks this.

2. C: They cloned a sheep

They were the first team to succeed in cloning a mammal. Dolly the sheep was named after Dolly Parton on account of being cloned from a mammary gland cell.

3. C: Coins

The Iron Agers made the first coins to be minted in Britain but rejected the idea of contactless card payments as 'too much like druid sorcery'. Not.

4. B: Voting rights for the working class

In 1839, a petition signed by 1.3 million working people failed to win even a parliamentary debate about voting rights for workers, and violence soon followed.

5. B: She was accused of adultery

With five men including her own brother. Most historians believe that she was innocent, and that it was Henry who put it about and slept not only with her own sister but also possibly with her mother. What really caused her undoing was that she couldn't give Henry the male heir he wanted, although she did bequeath to the nation a daughter destined to become one of history's most iconic monarchs, Elizabeth I, Gloriana.

6. D: Carrots

But intestines *are* included in the recipe, as per Robert Burns's 'Address to a Haggis': 'Painch, tripe, or thairm' (stomach, tripe, or intestines).

UK Citizenship Level: ANSWERS

7. C: 1973

Prime Minister Edward Heath would later describe it as 'the most enthralling episode in my life!'

8. A: He served in the RAF

As a fighter pilot. Dahl was lucky. He trained with 15 other men at the outbreak of the Second World War. Thirteen of them were killed in action within two years.

9. FALSE

If you are older than 70, you won't be invited to be a juror, even though you are on the electoral register and are allowed to vote.

10. B: Queen of the Iceni tribe who fought the Romans

Boudicca's uprising wreaked havoc in what are now London and St Albans, but she was defeated by the Romans at the Battle of Watling Street in AD 60 and probably took her own life. Her poignant speech to her troops before the start of battle spoke of rape and sexual abuse by the Romans: 'I am avenging lost freedom, my scourged body, the outraged chastity of my daughters. Roman lust has gone so far that not our very persons, nor even age or virginity, are left unpolluted. But heaven is on the side of a righteous vengeance.'

11. B: *The Mousetrap* by Agatha Christie

It opened in 1952 and is still running after more than 25,000 performances. Film producers have queued up to adapt it, but the original contract states that the theatre production must be closed for six months first.

12. C: MLAs

(Members of the Legislative Assembly)

13. A and C: Putting out refuse bags in communal areas or on the street when it's not bin day, and allowing your garden to become untidy

But please don't let that make you believe that sleeping with your neighbour's wife won't cause a problem.

14. D: Technically, *The Archers*

But for those in the know, *The Archers*, the world's longest-running radio drama, is certainly a national, if not constitutional, institution.

15. B: The founding of the Sikh order

It is also the Sikh New Year and is celebrated on 14 April with parades, singing and dancing. The story is that in 1699, Guru Gobind Singh challenged any Sikh who was prepared to give up his life to come into his tent. One man stepped in, and the Guru came out again carrying a bloody sword. Another man came forward, and the same thing happened. After five men had disappeared into the tent, the crowd became agitated, but then the Guru came out again with all five men alive and well, each sporting a turban. These five men became known as the Beloved Five, the first to be baptized as Sikh warriors to defend religious freedom.

16. A: To keep the Picts out

Could this be the etymological source of the phrase 'the picket line'?

17. B: The Beveridge Report

It recommended ways of fighting 'the five Giant Evils of Want, Disease, Ignorance, Squalor and Idleness' – setting the tone for what was to become the welfare state.

18. A: He was the first Englishman to circumnavigate the globe

The first ever to circumnavigate the earth is usually said to be Portugal's Ferdinand Magellan in 1522, even though he died before completing the journey. Drake's voyage was undertaken between 1577 and 1580. On his return, Elizabeth I knighted him but demanded, on pain of death, that all written accounts of the voyage became 'secrets of the Realm'.

19. C: More than ten hours a day

That means they could work as little as 70 hours a week. However, the Victorians were very relaxed about the gig economy.

20. B: The monarch

The Queen formally appoints the government, which the people have chosen via an election.

21. A: A Justice of the Peace Court

Major criminal cases as well as many civil cases are tried in a Sheriff Court, while the most serious crimes are heard in a High Court.

22. D: Their licence is only renewed for three years at a time (instead of ten)

There is no compulsory eye test for the over 70s, but you could be prosecuted 'if you drive without meeting the standards of vision for driving', according to the DVLA. Which of course will be hard to do if you've killed yourself by crashing into a lamppost you didn't spot.

23. C: Gustav Holst

In spite of the Teutonic name, Holst was born British.

24. B: Roman Catholic religious services were banned in Scotland

This is sometimes known as the Scottish Reformation. This obviously caused problems for the devoutly Catholic Mary, Queen of Scots, who returned to take up the throne of the newly Protestant Scotland after being widowed at just 18. After being forced to abdicate in 1567, she descended on her cousin Elizabeth I, only to be imprisoned after becoming the focus of several Catholic plots to snatch the English Crown. She was executed in 1587.

TEST

6

UK Citizenship Level: ANSWERS

1. B and C: Scotland and Northern Ireland (St Andrew's Day on 30 November and St Patrick's Day on 17 March)

In England, there is no public holiday to celebrate national identity, although there have been petitions to declare St George's Day a bank holiday.

2. A and C: They didn't read the Bible in Latin, and they did not pray to saints

Yes, these really were sins for which Protestants were burned at the stake. Freud's phrase 'the vanity of small differences' springs to mind.

3. B: George Frederick Handel

Handel wrote it for King George II. *Life in the UK* is quick to point out that although Handel was born in Germany, he spent many years in the UK and became a British citizen.

4. B: A Roman fort (and a part of Hadrian's Wall)

In the 1970s, archaeologists discovered Roman letters (written on wood), now known as the Vindolanda tablets. In one, a Roman cavalry officer called Masculus asks his superiors to supply more beer.

5. FALSE

The rebellion was crushed and the ringleaders executed. Ireland did not become a republic until 1949.

6. B: It doubled from one to two million

In 1934, the highest ever number of road casualties was recorded – 7,343 deaths and 231,603 injuries. Minister of Transport Leslie Hore-Belisha called it 'mass murder', as speed limits had been removed by the previous government He became responsible for the 30-mile speed limit in built-up areas, the Belisha beacon at pedestrian crossings, and for introducing the driving test.

7. B: He ran a mile in under four minutes

His record lasted all of 46 days, and he achieved it with little training while practising as a junior doctor. Try to find a junior doctor with four minutes to spare today, eh?

8. A: Catherine of Aragon, Anne Boleyn, Jane Seymour, Anne of Cleves, Catherine Howard, Catherine Parr

As any schoolchild knows, Divorced, Beheaded, Died; Divorced, Beheaded, Survived. Yes, it is a requirement of the citizenship test that you know the order of these marriages – after all, you never know when, as a loyal citizen, you might need it.

9. B: Towns and cities

As voting rights were still reserved for men owning property, members of the working class continued to be disenfranchised.

10. C: A radio telescope

Once the biggest in the world, it was built by Sir Bernard Lovell in 1945 in Cheshire and is still in operation today.

11. D: Penicillin

Fleming won the Nobel prize for his discovery, and *Life in the UK* tells us it is still used to treat bacterial infections today. But with the advent of superbugs, for how much longer is the question.

12. B: Clement Attlee

Many expected Churchill, a war hero, to win. However, Labour secured a landslide on a social-reform ticket. Attlee famously told his ministers: 'You will be judged by what you succeed at, gentlemen, not by what you attempt.'

TEST 7

UK Citizenship Level: ANSWERS

13. D: Both are equally responsible

But – be honest – which one of you is leafing through this quiz book while the other is putting the kids to bed?

14. C: 25 per cent

Although a majority of Brits identify themselves with a religion, fewer than 10 per cent are regular worshippers.

15. C: The prime minister, acting through the Queen

The Crown Nominations Commission supplies two names to the prime minister, who selects one to present to the Queen. Your starter for ten: do you know the name of the current archbishop? (Justin Welby)

16. A: Parliament wouldn't give Charles I money to fight the Scots and Irish

Parliament objected to Charles imposing reforms on the Church, which had also led to the Scottish unrest. As for the Irish, they were, as always, restless.

17. D: Recruiting workers to emigrate to the UK to drive buses

One Barbadian bus conductor, Ruel Moseley, remembers what it was like when he first came to the UK: 'You were not used to sharing five to a room. However poor you were in Barbados, you were not used to sharing a room. You had to be in work by 6.30 a.m. You had to keep your dignity . . . you had to keep working . . . A lot of boys came here and had mental breakdowns because of that stress.'

18. B: To mark a time of sexual and social liberation and the emergence of a distinct British pop music and fashion culture

As the famous saying goes: 'If you can remember the sixties, you weren't really there.'

19. C: Angles and Saxons

The languages spoken by the Angles and Saxons became the basis of modern-day English.

20. C and D: By contacting the Education Service or an MLA

Yes, *Life in the UK* really wants a prospective British citizen to check they understand exactly how they can go about arranging a visit to Stormont, Westminster, Holyrood and the Senedd, regardless of where they live and whether or not they might be interested.

21. C: 16

The other 36 countries in the Commonwealth must manage without her.

22. B: Plant life from around the world is showcased

As Tim Smit, the man behind the Lost Gardens of Heligan as well as the Eden Project, has said: 'A garden is a symbol of man's arrogance, perverting nature to human ends.'

23. C: The franchise

Although *Life in the UK* insists this is so, everyone else seems to call it the electorate. These days a franchise is surely understood to be a branch of McDonald's at an airport.

24. C: Unlike France or America, revolutionary movements in the UK have never led to a permanent and complete change in the system of government

'The British Constitution has always been puzzling and always will be' – Queen Elizabeth II

T
E
S
T

7

UK Citizenship Level: ANSWERS

1. B: The monarch is appointed by God and can rule without consulting Parliament

King Charles I was a believer in the Divine Right of Kings until Parliament taught him a lesson the hard way – by cutting off his head.

2. C: Pay As You Earn – PAYE

'Put simply, the state educated me, fixed my leg when it was broken, and gave me a grant that enabled me to go to university. It fixed my teeth (a bit) and found housing for my veteran father in his dotage . . . It has never been hard for me to pay my taxes because I understand it to be the repaying of a large, in fact, an almost incalculable, debt.' – Zadie Smith

3. D: Sir Robin Knox-Johnston

Drake didn't sail alone. Chichester had circumnavigated the globe two years earlier but stopped en route.

4. C: Newmarket

'Horses are red, Horses are blue, Horses that lose are turned into glue . . .' – Anon

5. A and B: Banking and weaving

They were Protestants who were persecuted in France for their religious beliefs, and many of them were educated and highly skilled.

6. B: The right to retain their own earnings and property

Another Act, the 1873 Infant Custody Act, increased mothers' rights over their children, including the possibility of custody after divorce.

7. D: Subsidized MPs' bar in the House of Commons

It is comforting to note, however, that there are now at least eight subsidized bars in the Palace of Westminster today.

8. B: Denmark

According to the ever-reliable *1066 and All That*, the unfortunately named Cnut, more commonly known as Canute, came to the throne after 'Ethelread [the Unready] was taken completely unawares by his own death' and Canute, 'having set out from Norway [*sic*] to collect some Danegeld, landed by mistake at Thanet, and thus became King.'

9. D: Sir John Lavery

As well as Queen Victoria, Belfast-born Lavery also painted Michael Collins, leader of the Irish independence cause and member of the IRA. Lavery's second wife Hazel modelled as the female personification of Ireland which appeared on Irish banknotes until the euro was introduced in 2002.

10. A: A power station

The museum is housed in Bankside Power Station, which produced electricity from 1891 to 1981.

11. C and D: Deer and horses

According to *Life in the UK*, both were eaten, though it wouldn't be such a surprise to find that they ate wild boar as well when they could track one down. The UK horse-meat scandal was still several millennia away.

12. C: The Bill of Rights, 1791

After America declared independence from British rule, Congress ratified the US Bill of Rights in 1791. But as pointed out in *Life in the UK*, British diplomats and lawyers did play an important role in drafting the European Convention on Human Rights and Fundamental Freedoms, and the UK was one of the first countries to sign the Convention in 1950.

13. B: To use up eggs, fat and milk before fasting during Lent

'Shrove' means atonement through confession and doing penance. This is a rather puritan and frugal British version of the bacchanalian feasting, drinking and wild partying that happens in other parts of the Christian world on the same day on Mardi Gras, 'Fat Tuesday'.

14. C: The largest empire the world has ever seen

Life in the UK states that the Empire had an estimated population of over 400 million and that the British were encouraged to emigrate overseas, with 13 million citizens leaving the country between 1853 and 1913.

15. B: *Under Milk Wood*

Set in a small Welsh fishing village called Llareggub, the tone of the work is set when you try reading that name backwards.

16. C: 'From cradle to the grave'

This was the phrase in the Beveridge Report which set out the principles of the welfare state for Clement Attlee's Labour government. In fact, the idea of the welfare state was first introduced by arch-conservative German Chancellor Otto von Bismarck, who used it to keep German workers from joining the Socialists.

17. D: He hid in an oak tree.

Defeated by Cromwell, Charles then escaped to the Continent disguised as a servant. When he returned nine years later, he was still only 30 years old.

18. B: A criminal offence

But an arranged marriage where both parties agree to the union is quite legal under British law.

19. TRUE

Even though Liechtenstein, Iceland and Norway are not in the EU, driving licences from these countries are valid in the UK along with all EU licences.

20. C: The potato crop failed.

The question is why the Irish poor relied so much on potatoes as their main crop. Some say it is because they were easy to grow on small plots. Others say that it's the only crop that can produce chips. If Marie Antoinette had been there, she would have suggested they eat cake.

21. B: The power to advise, warn and encourage

She used to have the right to dissolve Parliament and call a general election but not since the Fixed-terms Parliament Act of 2011.

22. C: Rugby league

The sport emerged in the late nineteenth century after a split with rugby union. Working-class players from northern English towns rejected union's amateur rules since they couldn't afford time off to play or train without payment like their wealthier southern counterparts.

23. B: The overthrow of King James II and accession of William and Mary without violence

Perhaps calling it the 'Glorious Revolution' was a way of obscuring the fact that this, instead of 1066, was the last successful invasion of Britain by a foreign power.

24. B: Gilbert and Sullivan

It is true that laughing at ourselves and our institutions has a proud tradition: 'When Britain really ruled the waves / (in good Queen Bess's time) / The House of Peers made no pretence / To intellectual eminence / Or scholarship sublime'.

T E S T 8

UK Citizenship Level: ANSWERS

1. B: The Prophet Ibrahim being prepared to sacrifice his son at God's request

Not to be confused with the better-known Eid al-Fitr, which marks the end of a month's fasting amid much feasting, Eid ul-Adha reminds Muslims of their own commitment to God through the story of Ibrahim's willingness to sacrifice his son.

2. A: He was buried in his ship with his treasure

The king is widely believed to be Raedwald, who ruled East Anglia in the seventh century.

3. B: The resolve in adversity shown during the evacuation of Dunkirk

Churchill called the evacuation of over 300,000 British and French troops cornered at Dunkirk a 'miracle of deliverance', but later countered the over-the-top public jubilation with a caution: 'Wars are not won by evacuations'.

4. D: Wales got its own parliament

The 1998 Act led to the establishment of the National Assembly for Wales in 1999, after the Welsh devolution referendum narrowly approved devolution. But *Life in the UK* also mentions an earlier Act for the Government of Wales, during the reign of Henry VIII, under which Wales was united with England.

5. TRUE

St Augustine was sent by Pope Gregory to establish an English church in AD 595.

6. B: Preston Bypass

This was Britain's first section of motorway and was opened in 1958, 99 years after Brunel's death.

7. A: Every September or October

This is according to *Life in the UK*, although other sources claim the register is updated in real-time between January and September every year.

8. C: The Moderator

The Church of Scotland website explains: 'The Moderator is not the head of the Church: the Church of Scotland holds that Jesus Christ is "the King and Head of the Church", nor is the Moderator the leader of the Church of Scotland, or its spokesperson.'

9. A: She is a Paralympian holding 11 Paralympic gold medals

She also won the London Marathon six times and set over 30 world records.

10. B: Its members are elected by the people

The Lords, on the other hand, except for the remaining hereditaries, are appointed via the Queen by the prime minister.

11. D: One of the Pre-Raphaelite Brotherhood

One of Millais' most famous paintings is of *Hamlet*'s Ophelia lying drowned in her watery grave. For realism, he got his model to lie in a cold bath for hours, resulting in her catching, if not pneumonia, at least a bad cold.

12. D: Ireland

The Ireland Act of 1949 established Eire as a separate country outside of 'His Majesty's dominions'. However Northern Ireland was not included, sowing the seeds for much future discord.

13. A: The prime minister

The first man to be called prime minister was Sir Robert Walpole in 1721, although at the time it was an unofficial and even derogatory term (it suggested improper autocracy, and Walpole himself, when accused of this, declared: 'I unequivocally deny I am sole and prime minister'). The premier's official title was First Lord of the Treasury, until 1905 when the term prime minister was first used in the official order of parliamentary precedence.

14. A: Small Scottish farms were destroyed to make way for large flocks of sheep and herds of cattle

Life in the UK points out that there were large-scale evictions, causing many Scots to emigrate to America in the nineteenth century.

15. B: That freedom of religious and political belief was a human right

One of the greatest eighteenth-century Enlightenment thinkers calling for religious and political freedom was a Frenchman who lived for a time in exile in England. Voltaire's works were widely read, not least *Candide* ('One must cultivate one's garden').

16. A: To restore Catholicism to England

Sellar and Yeatman called the Armada 'the Great Spanish Armadillo'. Which is almost on the way to Amarillo.

17. B: A piece of music by Benjamin Britten

Based on a composition by Purcell, it was written to introduce children to the different instrument sections of the orchestra.

18. C: Represent lobbyists' views in the chamber for a fee

MPs may not act as paid advocates for lobby groups. Nor is cash for questions allowable, or at least not since the scandal involving Neil Hamilton and Mohamed Al-Fayed broke in the 1990s.

19. TRUE

Its ingredients are bacon, eggs, sausage, black pudding, white pudding, tomatoes, mushrooms, soda bread and potato bread. You could get a heart attack just thinking about it.

20. A: The Department for Work and Pensions

A foreigner can start work without a National Insurance number, and obtain one from the DWP, but being granted a National Insurance number does not on its own confirm that they have the right to work in the UK.

21. C: Shot to nothing

This is a term used in snooker. It ain't cricket.

22. B: He split the atom, which led to the development of the atomic bomb

He was actually born in New Zealand, but he led a team of Cambridge scientists, and we do like to claim any immigrant who has achieved greatness as one of our own.

23. B: She persecuted Protestants

A devout Catholic, Mary wasn't having anything to do with her father Henry VIII's Church of England, and her reign started out in a very bloody fashion. Fortunately, she died soon after coming to the throne, allowing her half-sister Elizabeth I, a Protestant, to take the Crown.

24. C: A film

The 1949 Ealing comedy is a fantasy in which residents of Pimlico in London seek independence from the British government amid post-war rationing and austerity. After Brexit, such unilateral declarations of independence from fed-up communities could well become a reality.

Section 1: Test 10

1. C: It is illegal for them not to

Broadcaster impartiality is laid down by law. These specific rules to ensure that broadcasters do not take sides do not apply to newspapers, for some unstated reason.

2. B: Impose a revised Prayer Book on the Scots

Charles's actions fuelled a rebellion which eventually led to the Civil War, and ultimately to his own execution. Hardly surprising: how would we like it if the Queen tried to impose, say, Harry Potter and the Chamber of Secrets on the populace?

3. B: Four million

And yet we still managed to produce William Shakespeare.

4. D: Gurdwara

The authors of *Life in the UK* are so keen to make sure you understand that religions other than that of the Church of England are practised in the UK that they like to throw in this kind of arcane detail.

5. D: He achieved them all in a wheelchair

Weir was born with a congenital condition which denied him the use of his legs.

6. C: Alfred the Great

Yes, he of the cakes. Not so clumsy after all.

7. C: Fifteenth-century Scotland

Golf's Scottish origins may help to account for the puzzling fashion for golfers to wear wildly checked tartan trousers.

8. D: Discrimination in the workplace

This comes under employment law, which is part of civil law not criminal law.

9. B and C: They might feed your pets when you are away, and they might offer advice on local shops

These are obviously typically British forms of behaviour that the Home Office considers foreigners will never have encountered before arriving in Britain.

10. FALSE

Only British, Irish and Commonwealth citizens may vote in a General Election. But EU citizens can vote in all local and EU elections. Americans in Britain don't get a vote at all.

11. D: Alimentum (Roman food)

Although they are credited with introducing vegetables like the onion and the cabbage to Britain, many Roman delicacies failed to catch on – for example, stuffed dormouse.

12. FALSE

Rape is rape and is against the law.

13. B: Steam

'It is arguable whether the human race have been gainers by the march of science beyond the steam engine' – Winston Churchill

14. A: Wales was annexed to England

And just to make sure the Welsh got the message, Edward I built Caernarvon castle to enforce his new power.

15. C: The French

The war, which was about the succession to the French throne, actually lasted for 116 years, from the middle of the fourteenth century to the middle of the fifteenth. One battle, the Battle of Crécy, was provoked by French troops mooning an English detachment. Some say this war set the tone for the suspicion and hostility with which the English and the French have viewed each other ever since.

16. C and D: India and Singapore

The East India Company at one time controlled almost half the world's trade in basic commodities like tea, cotton, silk and even opium. It was a bit like Amazon except it didn't leave parcels of opium behind your rubbish bin and, if you didn't like the terms of business, it had its own private army.

17. C: Leamington Spa

The first tennis club was founded in Royal Leamington Spa in 1872. Wimbledon had started off as a croquet club and only changed its name to the All England Croquet and Lawn Tennis Club in 1877.

18. TRUE

Together with civil servants, members of the police, convicted criminals, judges and 'government-nominated directors of commercial companies'.

19. D: Fifteen

It is the only jury of its kind in the world not to rely on 'Twelve good men and true'.

20. A: Sir William Walton

The orchestral march played at the Queen's coronation in 1953 was called 'Crown Imperial' and was originally written for the coronation of the Queen's uncle, Edward VIII. After the latter's abdication, her father George VI was crowned on the day that had been planned for his brother's coronation, and the march was first played then. It was also heard at the wedding of Prince William and Catherine Middleton in 2011.

21. B: EEC (European Economic Community)

The 1957 Treaty of Rome sealed the European Economic Community set up by France, Germany, Belgium, the Netherlands, Italy and Luxembourg. The UK did not want to join even though the idea had originally come from Churchill. It finally joined in 1973 and has wobbled about its membership of what has become the EU ever since.

22. A and B: Hans Holbein the Younger, and Anthony van Dyck

Holbein was German and Swiss, and painted a famous portrait of Henry VIII. Van Dyck was Flemish and painted Charles I. Turner was born British, and Rembrandt remained in Holland.

23. B: The adventures of a group making a pilgrimage to Canterbury

Chaucer was the first writer to be buried in Westminster Abbey. Not because he was a poet, but because he was Clerk of Works in the Palace of Westminster.

24. C: A list of all those resident in every English town and village after the Norman Conquest, plus their animals

'After reading the book through carefully William agreed with it and signed it, indicating to everybody that the Possessions mentioned in it were now his' – *1066 and All That.*

UK Citizenship Level: ANSWERS

1. A, B and C: Dame Judi Dench, Sir Anthony Hopkins and Colin Firth

The test requires that you know this, but *Life in the UK* doesn't mention that Hopkins became an American citizen in 2000.

2. FALSE

Henry did proclaim himself King of Ireland, but it was not the will of the Irish people. The attempted imposition of Protestantism in Ireland led to centuries of unrest.

3. A: Denmark and Norway

The first recorded attack on the British mainland was in 789 when Norwegian Vikings landed on the Isle of Portland in Dorset. But one thing the Vikings did not bring to the stiff-upper-lip Brits was the cosy Danish concept of *hygge*.

4. FALSE

Thanks to the efforts of Gruffydd ap Cynan in Wales, the Normans failed to gain a lasting stronghold there, and they didn't manage to conquer Scotland either.

5. C: The Harrier jump jet

Was a marvel of UK aeronautical engineering in the 1960s. However, it went out of production in 2003. In 2011, one was available for purchase on eBay for £70,000.

6. C: Scotland defeated the English to remain independent

Robert the Bruce defeated the forces of Edward II in a brutal two-day battle. Emboldened, he later tried to invade Ireland, unite it with Scotland, and thus establish a 'Pan-Gaelic Greater Scotia'. It is still unclear if a Pan-Gaelic Greater Scotia football team would ever have qualified for the World Cup.

A

7. C: You must show photo ID before voting

Despite allegations of low-level voter fraud in the 2017 General Election, it is still not mandatory to show ID at polling booths elsewhere in the UK.

8. D: The king gave lands to his lords; in return, they provided peasant soldiers for his wars

There were three classes of peasant in medieval England: the slave, serf and villein. All lived under the protection of their lord in exchange for labour and serving as soldiers. The villein had most rights, but even he needed permission from his lord to leave the manor or even marry. However, he did have the right to refuse zero-hour shifts at Sports Direct.

9. B: *Brief Encounter*

It was adapted from a Noel Coward play. Laura, a married woman, gets some grit in her eye while sitting in a train station café. A passing doctor, Alec, also married, helps her. They go to the cinema but they don't even snog. Nevertheless, wracked with guilt, Alec accepts a job in South Africa while Laura considers jumping in front of a train. You can see why they call the British repressed, can't you?

10. A: Setting the strategic direction for the school

But not necessarily its religious direction. In 2015, the 'Trojan Horse' scandal (where it was alleged that school boards in the Birmingham area had been infiltrated by Islamist extremists) led to a call for a national register of school governors.

11. B: He was a journalist

In the 1890s, Churchill was a war reporter for the *Daily Graphic*, the *Daily Telegraph* and the *Morning Post*. He covered wars in Cuba, India and Africa. In 1898, he took part in a cavalry charge at the Battle of Omdurman in Sudan and reported the enemy 'stabbed and hacked with savage pertinacity'.

TEST 11

UK Citizenship Level: ANSWERS

12. D: Not Proven

The verdict Not Proven is only available in a Scottish court and dates from the eighteenth century. These days Not Proven is roughly the equivalent of an English acquittal, suggesting if not innocence then a lack of sufficient evidence.

13. C: It is one of the earliest poems written in the Scots language

Barbour's poem *The Bruce* commemorated the Battle of Bannockburn.

14. D: 2011

The Welsh Assembly was formed in 1999 but has only been able to make laws in certain limited areas without the agreement of the UK Parliament since 2011.

15. C: The world's finest products and inventions

It was actually called the Great Exhibition of the Works of Industry of All Nations. As a flier advertised: 'Come to the Exhibition / Sweet Catherine with me / And for a bob a piece my love / Such funny things we'll see'.

Six million visitors attended over five months and tour operator Thomas Cook arranged travel for Britons outside London. The huge plate-glass exhibition hall designed by Joseph Paxton was later dismantled and moved to Penge Common in south London, the area later becoming known as Crystal Palace.

16. A: Valid everywhere in Britain

But that doesn't mean shops and businesses have to accept them. A very British conundrum.

17. B: The Restoration

It used to be marked as a public holiday called Oak Apple Day or Royal Oak Day, when people wore oak leaves or oak apples. Those who failed to obey the custom were liable to be whipped with nettles or pinched on the bottom. Held on 29 May, it was abolished in

Victorian times, though apparently it is still celebrated today in some parts of the country, so on that day, do make sure to look behind you!

18. B: The right to a fair trial

Habeas Corpus literally means 'you have the body': 'you must present the person in court' – i.e. everyone has the right to a fair trial. This first passed into law in 1679. One of the act's provisions states that if a jailer is caught mistreating a prisoner he is liable to pay a large fine to his victim.

19. TRUE

She appoints, but she doesn't get to choose it: after a general election, she invites the leader of the party with the biggest number of MPs – or, where there is no majority, the leader of a coalition – to form a government.

20. A: He campaigned against the slave trade

The Slavery Abolition Act came into effect just over a year after his death in July 1833. Wilberforce, an evangelical Christian and Member of Parliament, was not a man for resting on his laurels. He turned down a peerage and also helped start the Society for the Prevention of Cruelty to Animals (later the RSPCA). 'Life as we know it, with all its ups and downs, will soon be over. We all will give an accounting to God of how we have lived,' he once said.

21. B: Hansard

Hansard has published transcripts of parliamentary proceedings and debates since 1909 and is named after Thomas Hansard, the first printer of such reports. Before 1771, publishing the debates was illegal and punishable by incarceration in the Tower of London. As a result, they were sometimes published heavily disguised under pseudonyms like 'Proceedings of the Lower Room of the Robin Hood Society and Debates of the Senate of Magna Lilliputia'. These days we keep a better eye on our rulers. TheyWorkForYou.com will tell you how your MP voted on key issues.

22. A: Britain, France and Turkey against Russia

Fear of Russian expansion in the Middle East led Britain and France to unite for a conflict which included the infamous Charge of the Light Brigade and saw the emergence of Florence Nightingale.

23. D: Bulgaria

Bulgaria joined the German side in 1915. Russia and France were British allies via the Triple Entente of 1907, which united the three empires (a response to the competing Triple Alliance of Germany, Austro-Hungary and Italy). However, Italy changed sides in 1915, and Japan supported Britain as a result of the Anglo-Japanese alliance of 1902.

24. D: There is no difference

The Good Friday Agreement was signed in Belfast in 1998, and the two terms are interchangeable. The agreement brought devolved government to Northern Ireland as part of a multi-party accord.

ANSWERS
Section 2: Order of Merit Level

1. C. Whale

There are recipes for whale as well as heron and swan. The scroll was compiled by 'the chief master cooks of King Richard II' and included pasta dishes too.

2. TRUE

And still in force via the Metropolitan Police Act 1839, as is a law prohibiting pubs and bars from serving drunk customers. Both laws are rarely enforced.

3. B: A model of the double-helix structure of DNA identified by Crick and Watson

The coach was a gift from an ardent Australian Royalist intended for the Queen's 80th birthday, but it was only finished eight years later; its first outing was for the State Opening of Parliament in June 2014.

4. C: 'Holder Born on an Aeroplane', would you believe?

No record is kept of whether Mum had the chicken, the beef or the vegetarian option.

5. B: People from Yorkshire

DNA studies show that people from Yorkshire have on average 41.17 per cent Anglo-Saxon DNA compared with a national average of 36.94 per cent. There's the proof that it really is God's Own County.

6. A: A nation of shopkeepers

Although whether Napoleon ever said this is a matter of dispute among historians. Nelson gave as good as he got – he is supposed to have said: 'There is no way of dealing with the Frenchman but to knock him down.'

7. B: The lands on the Continent ruled by English kings in the twelfth and thirteenth centuries

The Angevin Empire only lasted 60 years or so, but during it Henry II, Richard I and King John ruled more than half of France and Belgium as well as England, parts of Wales and Ireland.

8. C: A crossword puzzle in the *Daily Telegraph*

On 13 January 1942, the *Telegraph* ran a competition with a £100 prize for the winner to solve that day's crossword within twelve minutes. Several of the contestants were later contacted by a member of the General Staff inviting them to come and see them 'on a matter of national importance'. Several of the crossword boffins ended up working at Bletchley Park to break German codes.

9. FALSE

BBC current affairs show *Panorama* holds the record. It was first aired in 1953, even before the BBC News, which was launched a year later. *Coronation Street* first aired in 1960.

10. Any of them

During the late eighteenth century, the Industrial Revolution meant UK cities filled with the poor and destitute. British law rigorously defended property and, as a result, stealing anything valued at five shillings or more carried the death penalty. Transportation to Australia was introduced as a questionably more liberal punishment.

11. C: It made it illegal to handle a salmon in suspicious circumstances

In an attempt to stamp out illegal salmon poaching, the law gave police the authority to investigate any unusual handling of the fish.

12. C: 16

There is no firm law setting a minimum age for a babysitter. Yet unless the sitter is 16 or over, the parent is held legally responsible for the child's safety, so could be accused of putting their child in danger if anything went wrong. A British woman was cautioned by police in 2011 for leaving her 14-year-old son in charge of his three-year-old brother for 30 minutes.

13. A and C: Porpoises and whales

The Queen owns all the porpoises and whales as well as sturgeons in UK waters according to a statute going back to 1324 which is still valid today. But not many porpoises and whales know that.

14. C: Northern Ireland

Civil partnerships are legal and same-sex partners even have full adoption rights. However, same-sex marriage remains illegal.

15. FALSE

In 1812, George III's prime minister, the Tory Spencer Perceval, was shot dead in the lobby of the House of Commons by John Bellingham. Bellingham was a merchant with a grudge against the government, which he believed owed him compensation for time spent unjustly imprisoned in Russia. At his trial at the Old Bailey, Bellingham said that he would have preferred to have shot the British Ambassador to Russia. He refused to enter a plea of insanity and was hanged.

16. C: Vegetarians were angry because it contained animal tallow

Vegans and some religious groups were also upset – although it wasn't revealed from which animal the tallow came. But this time the country came off lightly – history tells us that pig or cow fat on bullets was enough to set off the bloody Indian Mutiny of 1857 in British India.

17. C: 'We see the absurdity of a small island imagining itself so important that the Continent should be isolated from it.'

Although the newspaper headline's existence is very much disputed, the Nazis seized on it to use in their propaganda, to show an arrogant and inward-looking British attitude to the Continent. The idea of Britain regarding itself as the fulcrum of the world is of course completely without foundation.

18. B: Radio 4's *Today* programme

Every British prime minister writes four handwritten 'letters of last resort' which are distributed to the commanders of four Trident nuclear submarines. The letters are to be opened when a submarine commander believes that Britain has suffered a devastating nuclear attack. One of the tests is whether Radio 4's *Today* programme has ceased to be broadcast. The *Today* programme went off-air for 15 minutes in 2004 following a studio fire alarm. Fortunately, no nuclear missiles were launched.

19. D: 25th

The UK ranked 25th behind Poland, Romania and Slovenia. Britain also saw the biggest difference between rich and poor children for consumption of healthy food, and one of the largest gaps in levels of physical activity between children from high- and low-income families.

20. A: Keeping Britain at a distance from all foreign entanglements

The term was coined by a Member of the Canadian Parliament George Foster, who noted with satisfaction: 'the great Mother Empire stands splendidly isolated in Europe'.

21. C: 12 miles

This is measured from the mark of low tide, and sovereignty extends to the air space above it as well as the seabed below.

22. C: The low-alcohol beer which was generally drunk by all in Britain, including children, from medieval times onwards

Small beer, or ale, was safer to drink than water, which was often stagnant and contaminated. That's not to say that it was safe to drink too much of it. Thomas Thetcher, who died in 1764, has this inscription on his tombstone: 'Here sleeps in peace a Hampshire Grenadier / Who caught his death by drinking cold small Beer / Soldiers be wise from his untimely fall / And when ye're hot drink Strong or none at all'.

23. B: A priest

Even while aboard HMS *Beagle* on his epochal voyage to South America, Darwin was a man of faith. He hoped to find 'centres of creation', but as the expedition progressed, his belief in the idea that species were created was shaken. However, forget that; you don't need to know that to be a British citizen. Neither Charles Darwin nor the theory of evolution gets a mention among the great British scientists and thinkers in the *Life in the UK* handbook.

24. D: Bath

In 827, Egbert, the first king to rule the whole of England, was crowned in the then capital Winchester. Colchester (or Camulodunum) was the Roman capital of Britain until it was moved to London. Tamworth was the capital of the Ango-Saxon kingdom Mercia.

Section 2: Test 2

1. B: Inner London East

In 2016, Eurostat, the EU's statistical agency, compiled a list of UK regions with people educated to degree level or higher; 58.3 per cent of people living in Inner London East (which includes the Canary Wharf financial centre) had a degree. North-eastern Scotland (which includes Aberdeen, a major oil-producing city with a university) scored 52.2 per cent, Outer London South 55.2 per cent and Oxfordshire, Bucks and Berks, despite the influence of Oxford University, only scored 51.7 per cent.

2. C: Down to the earth's core

However, before you start drilling, there are different laws governing mineral, oil and gas rights under the ground, as well as treasure.

3. D: Dorset

Men live to 82.9 years on average in East Dorset. Male Glaswegians live the shortest in the UK, with an average of only 72.6 years. In fact, according to the Office for National Statistics, only 75 per cent of Glaswegian males can expect to reach their 65th birthday. 'Be happy while you're living. For you're a long time dead,' goes the wise old Scottish proverb.

4. A: Nuneaton

Although it is the highest in the country, the teenage pregnancy rate has more than halved in Nuneaton since 1998. However, Britain still has one of the highest rates of teen pregnancy compared with other developed nations.

5. D: Diana, Princess of Wales

The poll was conducted five years after Diana's death, and the nation had not finished mourning. Others in the top ten included John Lennon, Elizabeth I (but not Elizabeth II for some puzzling reason), Horatio Nelson and Oliver Cromwell.

6. B: Seek medical attention

In Yorkshire dialect, a 'threp in't steans' is a kick in the testicles.

7. B: Your Majesty

According to Debrett's, you should call her Your Majesty first time round, and then, in the case of an extended conversation, address her thereafter as Ma'am (pronounced rhyming with lamb, not palm, 'which [sniff] has not been correct for several generations').

8. B: Aitken was sentenced to 18 months in prison

His case against the *Guardian* and Granada TV collapsed, and he himself was jailed for perjury and perverting the course of justice. While in jail he turned to Christianity and later published a book based on his experiences titled *Porridge and Passion*.

9. B: *Lady Chatterley's Lover* by D. H. Lawrence

In this 1960 trial at the Old Bailey against Penguin Books, Griffith-Jones told the jury that the book put 'lustful thoughts in the minds of those who read it', and his question about wives and servants brought derisory laughter from the spectators. The prosecution failed.

10. C: The founder saw the name in a dictionary and liked it

Company founder Joe Foster won a dictionary at a sports day when he was eight years old. When, in his twenties, he opened a cobbler's in Bolton, he called it Mercury but later changed it to Reebok after seeing the name of a South African gazelle in his dictionary. It has been claimed that Reebok invented the first spiked running shoe, but that is disputed.

11. D: They made Shakespeare popular by publishing his plays

Seven years after Shakespeare died, the pair, who had performed in his acting company, decided his plays ought to be collected and printed in a single volume, the First Folio.

12. C: Brandy or smelling salts

On 16 November 1898, the first moving staircase was inaugurated at Harrods' Brompton Road store; travelling on it for the first time was considered such a traumatic ordeal that staff stood ready at the top with remedies to treat giddy customers.

13. C: *Dictes and Sayinges of the Philosophres*

William Caxton may have printed earlier works, but this compendium of philosophers' sayings is the first English book printed with a colophon and dated – 1477.

14. A: Bristol

Cary Grant (born as Archibald Leach) grew up in poverty in Bristol, before moving to Hollywood and changing his name. As he said: 'Everyone wants to be Cary Grant. Even I want to be Cary Grant.'

15. C: 'One of the biggest mistakes of my career'

Although his government introduced the act, it came to be one of Blair's biggest regrets. He added: 'For political leaders it's like saying to someone who is hitting you over the head with a stick, "Hey, try this instead" and handing them a mallet.'

16. A: Cats

were not taxed, but almost everything else was. Mind you, when the Victorians started adding arsenic to wallpaper, it was probably good to have a deterrent to buying it.

17. A: Bang on the drum

More recently coined bingo calls include *Dancing Queen*, from Abba, for 17 and Theresa's Den, for ten.

18. D: Polish

According to the 2011 census, there are more than 500,000 Polish speakers in England and Wales. After that, Punjabi, Urdu and Bengali were most widely spoken. The least commonly spoken languages in England and Wales were Scottish Gaelic (58 people) and Manx Gaelic (33 speakers). Presumably there are more Gaelic speakers in Scotland, but the study doesn't tell us that.

19. B: Operation Sea Lion

The Germans planned to attack a broad stretch of the south coast and, after encircling London, move north to the 52nd parallel, roughly where Northampton is. They anticipated the rest of the country would then surrender.

20. B: Viagra (which was developed in Britain)

Taliban warlords tend to be elderly, with younger wives. A CIA informant told the *Washington Post*: 'Whatever it takes to make friends and influence people – whether it's building a school or handing out Viagra.'

21. C: An American ornithologist called James Bond

Fleming – a keen twitcher – owned a copy of *Birds of the West Indies* by James Bond and liked the name for its plainness. He said: 'I wanted the simplest, dullest, plainest-sounding name I could find, "James Bond" was much better than something more interesting, like "Peregrine Carruthers".'

22. B: Woking, Surrey

In Wells' novel, the 'inhuman, crippled and monstrous' aliens land on Horsell Common, north of Woking town centre, and respond to the greetings of curious locals by incinerating them with a heat-ray. Survivors then flee to nearby Leatherhead. Perhaps understandably, the 1953 Hollywood film moved the action to southern California, and the 2005 version starring Tom Cruise was set in New York.

23. B: Britain's history

Forty-five per cent of the people polled were proudest of their history. After that came pride in the NHS, then the Armed Forces, and last, but not least, the Royal Family.

24. A: 4.5 (according to the Office of National Statistics in 2017)

Fewer than you think? When questioned, most people's guess was closer to 24 unemployed in 100.

T
E
S
T

2

Order of Merit Level: ANSWERS

1. B: He wore an eyepatch

Nelson lost the sight in his right eye while fighting in Corsica in 1793 but never wore an eyepatch. Nor does his statue wear one on Nelson's Column.

2. B: The time at Sandringham, where clocks were set half an hour later than the rest of the country

This was instituted by Edward VII, so that he could go hunting without having to get up too early. Contrary to rumour, the clocks at Sandringham were not put forward to make sure the perpetually late Queen Alexandra was on time.

3. A: Beating a doormat in the street after 8 a.m.

This law sounds perfectly reasonable compared with some others still on the statute. For example, the 1839 law forbidding the flying of kites or sliding on ice.

4. B: Scotland and France would come to each other's aid if attacked by England

The Scotland–France alliance against England lasted until well into the sixteenth century and played a part in many conflicts including the Hundred Years' War.

5. C: That life on earth regulates its own environment

'Evolution is a tightly coupled dance, with life and the material environment as partners. From the dance emerges the entity Gaia,' Lovelock has said. However, his idea has been criticized by, amongst others, Richard Dawkins, who feels it contradicts evolutionary theory.

6. TRUE

The law treats a husband and wife as a single entity when considering conspiracy.

7. C: The Girls of Great Britain and Ireland Tiara

This curiously named tiara was given to Queen Mary in 1893 as a wedding gift by a committee of girls who raised the money to commission it from the jeweller Garrard. Queen Mary wrote that it 'will ever be one of my most valued wedding gifts'.

8. D: Only fish 'n' chips

can claim to be a wholly British invention, originating in London's East End Jewish community in the 1860s, and even then only by adding the chip to an already existing Portuguese/Spanish style of frying fish. St George was a Roman soldier of Greek origin probably born in Syria. The teabag was invented in New York. Pubs were invented by the Romans and originally called tabernae.

9. B: £4,550

London authorities dominate the list of highest per-pupil funding, with the City of London paying the most at £8,595 per pupil, ahead of Tower Hamlets (£7,014) and Hackney (£6,680.05). Cambridgeshire pays the least, at £3,950 per head.

10. C: Poor boys

Eton was founded as a charity to educate 70 poor boys. Today, the school fees will set a boy's parents back £37,062 per year.

11. A: 2,543

It was also only available from a stall at the north door of St Paul's Cathedral. There are now approximately 600,000 words in the *Oxford English Dictionary*.

12. D: Bring fire or flame into the library

You must also promise not to start a fire once inside. A valid warning, as a yearning for book-burning is a natural reaction for anyone being confronted with all those books.

13. C: Bongo

A more unfortunate spoonerism was from James Naughtie, who mispronounced then-Culture Secretary Jeremy Hunt's last name on Radio 4's *Today* programme in 2010 and then was heard having an uncontrollable fit of the giggles. The original eponymous Reverend Spooner was once heard to stumble over a toast to Queen Victoria, coming out with 'our queer old dean', and at a wedding, proclaiming that 'it is kisstomary to cuss the bride'.

14. B: Three Polish mathematicians

Polish mathematicians did crack the Enigma code in the 1930s and shared their information with the British. However, after the outbreak of the Second World War the Nazis began changing Enigma's cipher system on a daily basis. This was the challenge faced by Turing and fellow codebreaker Gordon Welchman at Bletchley Park.

15. C: Church Flatts Farm, Derbyshire

In Britain, you are never further from the sea than when you stand at Church Flatts Farm in Derbyshire, says the Ordnance Survey. Here, you are a full 70 miles from the nearest coast.

16. A: They triggered a tsunami which made Britain an island

These huge landslides started about eight thousand years ago, and probably knocked out the land bridge that had connected the British Isles to the continent of Europe. You could say this was the Mesolithic equivalent of our own Brexit.

17. C: None

The Queen was educated by a governess and the vice provost of Eton College but has no formal educational qualifications.

18. A: Build a shelter in a cupboard under the stairs

In Raymond Briggs' apocalyptic picture book *When the Wind Blows*, the elderly couple obediently follow this advice. It doesn't help them survive. 'Duck and cover' was the American version of civil-defence advice in case of a nuclear attack, although it did not go as far as suggesting you contort yourself to kiss your posterior.

19. TRUE

A 2016 survey by Ancestry DNA revealed that the average true Brit's DNA is a veritable European melting pot: 36.9 per cent Anglo-Saxon, 21.6 per cent Celtic, 19.9 per cent West European (Franco-German), 9.2 per cent Scandinavian, 3 per cent Iberian (Spain and Portugal) and 1.9 per cent Italian/Greek.

20. D: America

After that, in order, come France and Germany. Britain comes last, though we did consume 1.29 billion litres of the stuff in 2015, or 5.2 per cent of the world's wine, according to the Wine Institute.

21. TRUE

It is accessed through a plain white door near Terminal 5. The Foreign Office pays £100,000 for its upkeep a year plus a fee for each visitor.

22. B: Union Jack graffiti scratched onto the lunar module

A Union Jack was scratched onto an experiments package on the Apollo 11 lunar module by a British engineer.

TEST

3

Order of Merit Level: ANSWERS

23. A: A woman found a snail in her ginger beer while visiting a café in Scotland

In 1928, May Donoghue suffered gastroenteritis and shock after finding a snail in her ginger beer and sued the manufacturer. Though the ginger beer was bottled in dark glass (its contents could not therefore be inspected before consumption) and the woman had not even paid for it (a friend did), the case went to the House of Lords. Lord Atkin of Aberdovey ruled the drink maker owed a 'duty of care' to his customer and modern consumer rights were born.

24. C: Climbing a Scottish mountain

A 'Munro' is any Scottish mountain over 3,000 feet high. There are 282 in all and they were first climbed and classified by Sir Hugh Munro, who published details in *Munro's Tables* in 1891.

1. D: An NHS computer system failure

In 2002, the NHS announced it would go 'paperless' and keep patient records on the largest civilian IT system in the world. The project was abandoned in 2011 and the cost reached over £10 billion. The delayed Scottish Parliament building was also a pretty disastrous project with wildly escalating costs, but not on the same scale as the NHS one.

2. B: Brummies

A 2013 ITV survey found that 16 per cent of people from the Midlands have felt compelled to soften their accent socially or in the workplace. The Scots are least bothered. Only 2 per cent moderate their accent. Eight out of ten employers admitted making decisions based on accents.

3. A: A solar-powered plane that could stay airborne for three months

The company was Ascenta, an aviation consultancy which created Aquila, a plane that could stay airborne for months at a time and deliver internet signal to remote regions of the world.

4. C: Banknotes ripped accidentally

In order to qualify for a replacement, you must fill out a form and send at least 50 per cent of the damaged banknote to the Bank of England's rather marvellously named Mutilated Note Service based in Leeds.

5. B: EMI refused to grant permission for use of the song

One can speculate that EMI, the copyright holders, would be legitimately worried about aliens being able to listen to a Beatles song without paying for a licence.

6. A: After 9 p.m.

Lest the screams disturb the neighbours, presumably.

Order of Merit Level: ANSWERS

7. D: Don't give way to hating

The poem that inspired millions of British schoolboys was written by a man who himself had an unhappy childhood, being sent away to England at age five from India by his parents, where he was beaten and abused by the woman who was supposed to look after him.

8. C: A leg

Uxbridge's right leg was shattered above the knee near the end of the battle and amputated without anaesthetic at a house in Waterloo village. The householder Monsieur Paris buried the limb in his garden and it became a shrine visited by dignitaries including the King of Prussia. But the Uxbridge family literally gave more than an arm and a leg for their country, as Uxbridge's brother Edward also lost an arm fighting in Portugal, and his daughter a hand while nursing war wounded in Spain.

9. B: A rebellious cry against the King for not attacking the Spanish

In 1731, Spanish coastguards boarded an English merchant vessel and cut the ear off captain Robert Jenkins. This led to a diplomatic dispute and the song became a rallying cry for those demanding the King declare war against Spain. Over time, the song's lyrics were corrupted to suggest Britain was *already* pre-eminent (e.g. people tend to sing 'rules' the waves rather than the original 'rule', which was more of an exhortation to a future seizure of power).

10. B: Women with venereal disease be arrested and detained for up to a year

The Act was brought in to protect sailors on leave in ports, who were left free to spread their germs as they pleased.

11. B: It suggested methods of contraception

Annie Besant faced trial for the promotion of contraception, but the case against her collapsed due to a technicality. Yet the scandal caused by the case led to her losing custody of her children.

12. D: Seagulls

Tory MP Anne-Marie Trevelyan warned that people in her Berwick-upon-Tweed constituency had taken to the streets with firearms to kill seagulls after a series of attacks. 'There are people wandering the streets of Berwick with firearms who really shouldn't be doing so,' she noted. Oliver Colvile, MP for Plymouth Sutton and Devonport, added: 'As we head into the summer we could very well see gull wars on our high streets.'

13. C: 'First Lord of the Treasury'

The term prime minister was not officially used until 1905.

14. C: The Sweeney is slang for the police department featured in the series

Sweeney Todd is cockney rhyming slang for the Flying Squad, the Metropolitan Police's robbery and firearms investigation branch. Formed in 1919, it initially operated from a horse-drawn carriage touring London streets. Inside, policemen looked for street robbers through peepholes cut in the canvas awning.

15. B: The elite of the elite, drawn from all Special Forces (SAS, SBS and SRR)

E Squadron was formed in 2007 and is used to support the work of MI6. Its speciality is 'black ops', including 'military assistance to foreign governments', where, according to a Whitehall source, 'maximum discretion is required'.

16. D: Wessex owning a tobacco plantation in America

It is true that there were neither tobacco plantations nor British colonies in Virginia in the 1590s. But this anachronism isn't Shakespeare's, it comes from Marc Norman and Tom Stoppard's screenplay for the film *Shakespeare in Love*.

17. B: Suicide bombing

In June 1940, Churchill suggested to the Secretary of State for War that sticky bombs be used on German tanks by resistance fighters 'though its explosion cost them their lives'.

18. A: 17 years (according to the Ministry of Justice in 2016)

Only a small number of murderers have a 'whole life order' placed on them – meaning that 'life means life', and that they will never become eligible for parole.

19. C: Sold Nelson's Column to a tourist

Furguson is reputed to have sold it to an American tourist for £6,000 in the 1920s. He also took a £1,000 down payment for Big Ben and a further £2,000 for Buckingham Palace.

20. FALSE

They were sold to the Scottish Crown by Norway's King Christian I. He needed money for a dowry following the marriage of his daughter to James III of Scotland. He received 50,000 Rhenish guilders for Orkney and 8,000 for Shetland.

21. D: 96 per cent

According to the RAC, the average car spends about 80 per cent of the time parked at home and 16 per cent parked elsewhere. It is thus only actually in use (i.e. being driven) for the remaining 4 per cent of the time.

22. A: 'I'm the fall guy. I only blew £200 million.'

Leeson is reputed to have said this to a friend after losing £827 million. He is now a popular after-dinner speaker on risk and corporate governance, which earns him thousands of pounds for each appearance.

23. D: Diana, Princess of Wales

State funerals are reserved for the monarchy and other 'exceptionally distinguished persons'. Princess Diana was accorded only a 'ceremonial funeral', though a very public one at that. All the others, despite being 'commoners', were given a state funeral. After Churchill had a major stroke in 1953, secret plans had been formulated for his funeral under the code name Operation Hope Not, before his death in 1965.

24. A: 'Mrs Fanshaw from Chumley'

And don't let Mrs Woolfhardisworthy from Wybunbury put you off either. It's simply pronounced 'Mrs Woolsery from Win-bree'.

1. C: British Army target practice

The village was commandeered by the Army for target practice. A note on the church door reads: 'We shall return one day and thank you for treating the village kindly'. The 225 villagers never did go back.

2. B: Beethoven's Symphony No. 9

However, Mozart was the most requested artist from 1942 to 2011. No rock or pop artist has made the top ten in all 75 years of the Radio 4 programme.

3. B: *Honi soit qui mal y pense* (Shame on him who thinks badly on it)

Or, as *1066 and All That* translated it: 'Honey, your silk stocking's hanging down'. D is the Latin translation of 'To boldly go where no man has gone before' – *Star Trek*'s motto.

4. D: The tomb of the unknown warrior

The idea for the tomb came from the Reverend David Railton, who, while serving in France in 1916, noticed a makeshift grave in a back garden in the French town of Armentières. Its simple wooden cross was dedicated, in pencil, to 'An Unknown British Soldier'. In 1920, the idea was taken up and four bodies were exhumed from different First World War battlefields. A British general chose one at random to be taken back to England for re-burial, along with a sixteenth-century crusader's sword, in the abbey.

5. B: A temperate oceanic climate

Extraordinary how a normal temperate climate can be turned by the British into such an endless fund of daily agonizing and soul-searching chatter about the weather, hot or cold, wet or dry.

6. B: It invented a new form of fraud

During the financial crisis, the Bank of England offered loans to struggling banks via the Special Liquidity Scheme. In 2014, Lloyds was fined £105 million for attempting to rig the scheme which had been set up to help it.

7. B: Charles Dickens wrote *Oliver Twist*

However, barrister Amal Clooney does work at a Chambers based there, and Vera Brittain was once a resident of the street too.

8. D: *You're Barred, You Bastards*

Balon worked at the pub from 1943 to 2006 and was dubbed 'Britain's rudest landlord' for telling one customer, 'You're barred. You're too boring to be in my pub', and even more devastatingly to another, 'You're so ugly you're upsetting the customers'.

9. All of them

The British were known as 'les goddams' by the French during the Hundred Years War because they swore so much. The Romans called us Brittunculi or 'wretched little Britons'. The Germans dismissed us as 'Inselaffe', 'island ape'; and 'Limey' is an American nickname earned by nineteenth-century British sailors who sucked limes to fend off scurvy.

10. D: The government department collecting and allocating all revenues

The name supposedly derives from a medieval counting table, covered in a chequered tablecloth, on which early audits were done. These days the Exchequer draws money from the government's main bank account, called the Consolidated Fund, which is kept at the Bank of England.

11. B: 17 Bruton Street

The Yorks lived in a house in Bruton Street, Mayfair, which is now a Chinese restaurant.

12. A: Good health!

According to Geoffrey of Monmouth's twelfth-century *History of the Kings of Britain*, the guest was Hengist's daughter Renwein, and Vortigern thought her so charming he asked to marry her.

13. TRUE

A type of beef or lamb stew (formerly known as Lobscouse) eaten in Liverpool. Hence the term Scouser.

14. B: The Icelandic parliament

The English Parliament wasn't the first, it's the Johnny-come-lately, passing its first act in 1229. The Icelandic parliament, or Althingi, was founded in AD 930. The Isle of Man's Tynwald first sat in 979, and Ireland's first Act of Parliament was passed in 1216.

15. D: 1974

There have been women's colleges in Oxford since the nineteenth century, and women became full members of the university in 1920, but only in 1974 did five male colleges start admitting women students.

16. B: The Queen

The Channel Islands are the last part of the Duchy of Normandy to remain under the British monarch's rule. After disputes dating from Viking times, the rest of the Duchy was ceded to France in 1259.

17. D: One hundred million pounds

Not all banknotes are in general circulation. The Bank of England uses the £100 million note, or 'titan', for internal accounting purposes. There is also a 'giant' worth a piffling £1 million.

18. They can all be true

The child may be British if born in British airspace but can apply for American citizenship if born within US airspace (12 miles from the coast). Otherwise, the parents' nationality is the primary factor, although some airlines (e.g. Canadian) will offer babies born in-flight citizenship of their country too.

19. B: That it has been supplied to her household for at least five years

Current Royal Warrant holders include at least five separate 'purveyors of champagne' as well as the purveyors of HP Sauce. However, a member of the Royal Family may withdraw a warrant if displeased. HRH the Duke of Edinburgh withdrew his from Harrods in 2000 after what the Palace described as a 'significant decline in the trading relationship' between the Duke and the department store. In fact, then-Harrods owner Mohamed Al-Fayed had accused the Duke of masterminding the death of Diana, Princess of Wales, and his son Dodi Fayed. Al-Fayed eventually ordered the removal of all five Royal Warrants, claiming, 'Later, I had them burned. They were a curse, and business tripled following their removal.'

20. C: Helping the whips to make sure MPs are present for crucial votes

This is not a task for Black Rod. But he is responsible for security within the Palace of Westminster.

21. A: 5 foot 9.5 inches (177.6 cm)

British men have grown by 11 cm in height since 1916 and they are, on average, the 32nd tallest in the world. Dutch men are the tallest, at an average 5 foot 11 inches. Indonesian men are smallest, at an average 5 foot 2 inches.

22. C: Compulsory moustaches

Moustaches had been mandatory since the Crimean War. By contrast, the Royal Navy has never allowed moustaches unless grown with side whiskers attached.

23. All of them

They also ate larks and peacocks. It's a wonder there are any birds left.

24. A: Unpublished lines by Shakespeare

At the funeral of the Elizabethan poet Edmund Spenser, fellow writers including Shakespeare are rumoured to have tossed unpublished works into his coffin in tribute.

1. C: Someone else had reached the South Pole first

On arriving at the South Pole, they discovered that the Norwegian explorer Roald Amundsen had reached it 34 days earlier. Amundsen started 60 miles closer to the pole and used dogs, which were more resilient than Scott's ponies and oil-fuelled sledges. However, B and D also occurred. Scott's diary entry was poignant, but the worst was yet to come. On the way home, he and the four other team members with him died in a blizzard just 11 miles short of safety.

2. D: Shropshire

Dr William Penny Brookes, a Shropshire doctor, began the Wenlock Olympian Games at Much Wenlock in Shropshire in 1850. His intention was the 'physical and intellectual improvement of the inhabitants of the town' by means of 'outdoor recreation'. The cycling event was conducted on penny farthings. Baron Pierre de Coubertin visited the games in 1890 and was inspired to establish the International Olympic Committee four years later. The 2012 Olympic mascot was called Wenlock in honour of the town's role in creating the modern Olympics.

3. A: The price of the average UK house

By 1990, it had reached £60,000. By 2000, it was £109,000, and by 2013 it was £242,000.

4. A: The sitcom *Fawlty Towers*

As with many British sitcoms, the Americans tried remaking it for themselves and gave it this horrible title. *Chateau Snavely* was a disaster. Undeterred, they had another go, this time calling it *Amanda's*, and later another remake was titled *Over the Top*. All failed, and the original British version remains a cult favourite. Don't get us started on *Sanford and Son*, the pathetic US version of *Steptoe and Son*, or *The Rear Guard*, their highly questionable take on *Dad's Army*.

5. B: He suggested a link between the MMR vaccine and autism

Dr Wakefield's 1998 research on the MMR vaccine and autism published in the *Lancet* triggered a scare which led to a collapse in confidence in the vaccine, which resulted in a rise in cases of measles. His findings were later discredited, and he was struck off the medical register in 2010 for his research methods, which included paying children £5 for blood samples at his son's birthday party.

6. D: Australia

Australia has most British ex-pats, with 1,277,474 living there. America is second with 758,919. Canada has 674,371 and Spain has only 381,025.

7. C: Players' wages

According to the club's accounts, this was the total annual wage bill (including bonuses) for a team which included Denis Law, George Best and Bobby Charlton. When he left Manchester United in 2017 Wayne Rooney was being paid £260,000 a week or £13.52m a year.

8. D: Putting up a plaque in memory of a woman killed by a horse

It commemorates suffragette Emily Wilding Davison, who hid in the Palace of Westminster in 1911 so that she could record her address on the night of the Census as 'the House of Commons'. Two years later, she became a martyr to the cause of women's rights when she threw herself in front of the King's horse at the Epsom Derby. Benn claims to have put up several other such home-made plaques in the Houses of Parliament, adding that Davison's was: 'One of the few monuments to democracy in the whole building'.

9. C: Eurasian wolf

It still existed in the UK until 1680. The brown bear went extinct in AD 1000. Both the mammoth and woolly rhino have not been around since 10,000 BC.

TEST

6

Order of Merit Level: ANSWERS

10. C: A week of programmes about masturbation

They broadcast all the others, including two seasons of previously censored films and programmes in 1991 and 2004. However, the channel felt they would rub people up the wrong way with *Wank Week*, a week-long series of programmes about masturbation which was cancelled at the last minute in 2007. Then chief executive Charles Allen noted: 'That would be a hard one to pull off, even for Channel 4.'

11. B: A fair or market on the River Thames

Before the seventeenth century, London winters were far colder than they are now, and the Thames often froze solid for weeks at a time. The frozen river would become a street, with stalls stretching along it for miles. In 1683, one visitor to that year's frost fair described how 'a great street from the Temple to Southwark was built with shops and all manner of things sold'. He reported seeing bull-baiting, and a coach and six horses riding along the ice.

12. C: Cheese

When it became clear the fire might destroy his house, Pepys sent away his 'money and plate and best things' by cart and Thames barge. He then dug a hole with his friend Sir William Penn and 'put our wine in it and my Parmazan cheese'. Parmesan cheese had been highly valued since the Middle Ages.

13. C: A coinage first thought up by Walter Bagehot, a Victorian journalist

Bagehot stated that public opinion was best symbolized by 'the opinion of the bald headed man at the back of the omnibus'. Clapham was then an ordinary commuter suburb, and, with this detail added, the term soon came into legal use as an abstract measure of 'reasonable behaviour'. The concept has been adopted by other legal systems. In Melbourne, Australia, the equivalent is 'the man on the Bourke Street tram'. In Kenya, it is 'the man in the bush taxi'.

14. D: It is a centre for international money-laundering

The 'Global Laundromat' refers to the movement of an estimated $20-80 billion 'either stolen or with criminal origin' from Russia between 2010 and 2014. UK banks have been accused of playing a significant role in processing these payments, fuelling the capital's luxury property boom.

15. C: Its beach has been voted the best in Europe

It is also the only European beach in the world top ten, according to *Suitcase* magazine.

16. D: Peng

Meaning 'tasty, gorgeous'. 'Topping' is another British term signalling excellence but has fallen out of use. A and C are both American in origin.

17. C: Ugly Rumours

Blair sang and played guitar in the band while studying law at Oxford in the 1970s. Ugly Rumours only managed six gigs, possibly because Blair modelled his performances on Mick Jagger.

18. B: Four British spies

In the 1950s, the Venona Project, an American counter-intelligence programme, deciphered secret Russian messages which mentioned the existence of a British MI6 mole using the code name Homer. This was Donald Maclean, one of the original four spies. The others, Kim Philby (Stanley), Guy Burgess (Hicks) and Anthony Blunt (Johnson), were unmasked later.

19. D: A medieval bye-law governing the collection of firewood

Peasants were forbidden to chop down trees for firewood, on pain of severe punishment. However, they could gather wood which had already fallen if it was retrievable with a weeding hook or a shepherd's crook.

20. C: To do up her house

Buckingham Palace needs renovation. An official report warned of 'catastrophic building failure' after a workman used a wall-mounted pull-flush toilet and the entire unit came off the wall. The ten-year works will include replacing 2,500 radiators and 5,000 light fittings. A Palace spokesperson remarked: 'The boiler has not been replaced for 33 years', but it is unclear which member of the Royal Household he was referring to.

21. A: She didn't like their multicultural livery

In 1997, BA unveiled a set of tail-fin livery reflecting world cultures from the various countries they served. Mrs Thatcher disapproved and, while inspecting the new look designs, dropped her hankie over them, saying: 'We fly the British flag, not these awful things.'

22. C: A convention whereby what is said in a meeting can be reported as long as it is not attributed to anyone

The rule of non-attributable discussion. It came into existence in 1927 at London's Chatham House, headquarters of the Royal Institute for International Affairs. The idea was to promote free discussion, even if the opinions expressed were controversial. Those present were free to report what was said but not who said it.

23. D: Long-range telescopes

Most notably a phony BBC radio competition asked listeners to send in their best photos of holidays in northern France. These were used to draw a detailed picture of the proposed landing beaches. Two weeks before D-Day, the maps were distributed to the top brass, code named BIGOT (British Invasion of German Occupied Territory).

24. FALSE

But he did make a record with the Sex Pistols called 'No One Is Innocent'.

1. C: Celtic for 'knower of the oak'

'Dru' was the Celtic for oak and 'uid' meant 'one who knew'. The tree, and especially the oak, has had huge significance in Britain since ancient times. Oaks and their acorns were used for making ink, for tanning, feeding pigs and making wine and of course for building ships and houses.

2. D: Red Lion

There are over 600 pubs so called in the UK. The Red Lion featured on the crest of John O'Gaunt, Duke of Lancaster in the fourteenth century. Pub signs have had simple names accompanied by simple pictorials since medieval times when literacy levels were low. Drinkers could identify an inn or pub by the pub sign illustration alone. In these days of increased literacy, pubs with names like the Cock & Bull and Fanny on the Hill tend to be signposted without an image.

3. D: Drink, dance and have sex

They 'dance, drink and screw because there's nothing else to do'. Pulp singer Jarvis Cocker has said: 'I'm not saying that about every member of the working class, but I knew a lot of people who felt that way where I grew up in Sheffield.'

4. B: It was moved to Arizona

The bridge was deemed unfit for London traffic in 1967. An American property developer won it at auction for US $2.46 million in 1968. Robert P. McCulloch planned to erect it on an Arizona real-estate development called Lake Havasu City. Each granite block was carefully deconstructed, catalogued, shipped to California and then transported overland and rebuilt. It took three years and re-opened in 1971. According to popular rumour, it was bought on the mistaken assumption that it was the more familiar and iconic Tower Bridge, but this has always been denied.

5. FALSE

Greenwich Mean Time is so-called for a reason. It is only a 'mean' or an average. Sometimes noon GMT is out by up to 16 minutes. GMT was superseded as the international standard by Coordinated Universal Time, set by atomic clock, in 1972.

6. D: She was the first test-tube baby

When her mother was unable to conceive naturally due to blocked fallopian tubes, Dr Patrick Steptoe and Robert Edwards used a new technique called IVF to fertilize an egg artificially. Edwards later won a Nobel prize for his work. He pointed out that Brown was actually conceived in a petri dish not a test tube.

7. C: He made controversial comments about disabled people

Hoddle told a *Times* journalist: 'You and I have been physically given two hands and two legs and a half-decent brain. Some people have not been born like that for a reason. The karma is working from another life.' Hoddle was fired and his faith healer Eileen Drewery called the ensuing media furore 'a witch hunt'.

8. D: It refers to a weight of silver

Originally, a pound coin was so called because it weighed a pound of sterling silver (i.e. it contained at least 92.5 per cent silver). There were 240 pennies in a pound because 240 pennyweights made up a pound of silver. The £ sign is actually a corruption of the letter L, which stands for Libra, the Latin for pound.

9. C: She popularized tea as a drink

Tea had already been introduced to England before the Portuguese princess's arrival (Pepys mentions it as a new drink in 1660), but it was only when she turned up with a chest of the stuff and would drink a cup of it in preference to English ale that it became popular in the English court and thus socially.

10. C: Ryde

In fact, Ryde on the Isle of Wight is home to the world's first leisure pier. It opened in 1814 with a section for mooring ferries, and started a boom in pier construction. By 1914, 100 piers existed in the UK and 59 still survive today.

11. TRUE

The Queen posed the question at a charity function in 2014. Hawking explained that he writes on a computer via cheek movements which are detected by an infrared ray in his spectacles. Each sentence is then interpreted by a voice synth which, he reported, most people think sounds American, Scandinavian or Scottish.

12. D: Tinky Winky

The Teletubby was the only fictional character in the *Independent on Sunday*'s 2008 poll of 'a hundred people who give back, volunteer and who make Britain a better balanced happier country'. Tinky Winky had previously been criticized for being a young male carrying a handbag. In Poland, for example, the character was investigated on the grounds he might promote homosexuality to children but was exonerated.

13. TRUE

Frost died of a heart attack while working on a cruise ship in 2013. He was granted the memorial for his services to British culture.

14. D: Red grouse and ptarmigan

According to the Game Act 1831, these birds may be shot from 12 August (as long as it is not a Sunday) until 10 December each year. Oddly, black grouse have an extra week's grace (they can be shot from 20 August). Duck and goose may be shot from 1 September to 31 January. The shooting of grey heron and red-breasted mergansers is illegal, though the RSPB reported 44 attempts to kill these and other birds of prey in 2015.

15. A: Charlie Chaplin

Chaplin was hugely popular in 1930s Germany, but the Nazis denounced him in a 1934 book called *The Jews Are Looking at You* by Dr Johann von Leers. Chaplin took revenge with his first talking picture, *The Great Dictator* (1940), in which he played a Hitler-like demagogue. NB: it was generally assumed that Chaplin was Jewish, something he never denied, but although MI5 investigated him, nobody has ever found evidence that he was, or that he had been, as claimed, born into poverty in Britain.

16. B: By raising start-up funds through recycling stuff the royals didn't want

William Fortnum was a footman to Queen Anne and noticed that she insisted on new candles each evening. Wax was valuable, and he recycled her unused candles to help fund his grocer's business. He rented a spare room from Hugh Mason, and they went into business together in 1707. After they invented the Scotch egg in 1738 – a convenient takeaway snack for people travelling out of London – they never looked back.

17. C: He invented the adhesive postage stamp

in 1837, and by 1840 the Uniform Penny Post was in operation. Instead of a complex and corrupt system of postage whereby every parcel and letter required individual paperwork, the Uniform Penny Post meant a half-ounce letter could be posted anywhere in the UK for one penny, using the Penny Black stamp.

18. B: Vladimir Lenin

The Bolshevik leader was in exile in London. He convened a meeting under the guise of a barbers' convention. Fitch hid in a cupboard and heard him predict 'bloodshed on a colossal scale' in the new century.

19. A: English

Canadian graduates accrue an average £15,000 debt, Australians

£21,000 and Americans at not-for-profit universities £20,500. In England, £9,000+ fees, the abolition of the maintenance grant and 6 per cent interest rates on loans mean graduates leave with an average £50,000 debt.

20. B: Beer because it was English

In a pair of 1751 prints titled respectively *Beer Street* and *Gin Lane*, Hogarth portrayed residents of Gin Lane in London's Bloomsbury as dissolute, suicidal, prone to madness and even infanticide. By contrast, residents of Beer Street were full of health, joy and happiness. Beer was seen as wholesome and English, while gin, along with spirits generally, as foreign and corrupting.

21. B: *Eldorado*

Although its working title was *Little England*, the series aired as *Eldorado* from 1992. It told the story of a community of British ex-pats living in Spain, and it hoped to mix the gritty appeal of *EastEnders* with the sunnier aspects of successful Australian soaps like *Neighbours* and *Home and Away*. However, it was a disaster, criticized for amateur acting, ridiculous European accents and implausible storylines. It lasted a year. The set of the show in the Spanish town of Coin on the Costa del Sol is now used as a shooting range.

22. C: Two pandas

As part of what has been dubbed 'panda diplomacy' during the Cold War, the Chinese gifted two of the prized animals to Britain. Chia-Chia and Ching-Ching duly took up residence in London Zoo, but a row blew up over the expense of a special £70,000 panda enclosure, not to mention a daily supply of imported bamboo shoots. A Foreign Office report advised lack of panda hospitality could be viewed as a snub in Beijing, adding: 'Given the notorious sentiment of the British public about animals, this could make the government look unnecessarily unsympathetic'. The enclosure was built. Ching-Ching died in 1985, and Chia-Chia was then sent off to Mexico on permanent loan.

23. None of them

Mini and Rolls Royce are owned by German carmaker BMW (and Bentley is owned by German multinational Volkswagen). Jaguar and Land Rover are owned by the Indian firm Tata.

24. B and C: Wild boar and golden eagle

Wild boar are flourishing since being reintroduced 17 years ago. There are an estimated 1,000 in Kent, East Sussex and Gloucestershire. The golden eagle thrives in Scotland with 508 breeding pairs reported in 2015. There has been research done into the reintroduction of wolves into England and Scotland to help manage the deer population, but none have been introduced as yet. The lynx died out in AD 700, but there are plans to import six of the cats from Sweden into Northumberland in 2018.

Section 2: Test 8

1. C: Peeing in a policeman's helmet

Peeing anywhere in public, including in a policeman's helmet, is allowable for any pregnant woman. The other offences remain on the statute book.

2. C: Liverpool

The Yorkshire Devolution Movement currently campaigns for a separate legislature for the county, while Mebyon Kernow seeks an autonomous Cornish state. In Brighton & Hove, 8,000 people supported hat-maker Jason Smart's declaration of the People's Republic of Brighton & Hove following the 2015 Tory election victory. At present, there is no such independence movement in Liverpool, although a 2016 poll for the *Liverpool Echo* showed that 73 per cent of respondents would leave England and join Scotland if it gained independence. In fact, a petition to the UK government asking leave for Liverpool, Manchester, Leeds and Newcastle to secede and join a New Scotland currently has over 50,000 signatures.

3. D: FitzRoy

The others are all named after sandbanks. FitzRoy is named after Captain Robert FitzRoy, founder of the Met Office. Before that he was captain of the famous HMS *Beagle* during Charles Darwin's second voyage.

4. B: N.O.R.W.I.C.H.

'[K]Nickers Off Ready When I Come Home' is more lusty than romantic – although that's not to say wartime wives and girlfriends wouldn't have welcomed the sentiment. But it's a bit crude compared it to 'My Ardent Lips Await Your Arrival', 'Hope Our Love Lasts And Never Dies', or 'Sealed With A Loving Kiss'.

5. D: None of the above

It is a common misconception that there is such a thing as a common-law relationship that gives partners equal rights and entitlements to a married couple.

TEST 8

Order of Merit Level: ANSWERS

6. B: Alfred Hitchcock

Although he worked with Cary Grant on several movies, Hitchcock wasn't Grant's spymaster – that was Noël Coward. Although Hitchcock did contribute to the Allied war effort by making several propaganda films, he did not spy for British Intelligence, unlike the others in this list.

7. D: Deals with abandoned vessels or cargo at sea or washed up on beaches

All flotsam (goods lost from a ship), jetsam (goods thrown overboard), derelict (abandoned property including vessels) and lagan (goods cast overboard but buoyed for future recovery) must be reported to the Receiver of the Wreck. That old bit of wood the kids found on the beach at Margate? Technically, you should've reported it to the Receiver!

8. B: 'Posing as somdomite [sic]'

Wilde sued Queensberry, the angry father of his great love Lord Alfred Douglas, for libel, lost, was arrested for 'gross indecency with other male persons', and sentenced to jail, which inspired *The Ballad of Reading Gaol* – 'I never saw a man who looked / With such a wistful eye / Upon that little tent of blue / Which prisoners call the sky'.

9. B: One

Lloyd George is so far the only Welsh prime minister of Britain.

10. C: J. G. Ballard

This was the advice given by a publisher's reader about J. G. Ballard's *Crash* in 1973. Yet the novel was adapted for the screen by David Cronenberg and won the Special Jury Prize at Cannes.

11. A: One Penny

A penny for a groundling. Another penny for a seat, and another one for a cushion.

12. D: 'You can't abdicate and eat it.'

British history may dismiss her as 'that miserable, second-rate American woman', but it seems that Wallis had quite a witty side.

13. C: Being sacked over an extramarital affair

He wrote it in his *Telegraph* column of 2 December 2004 after being sacked as shadow arts minister. Never a truer phrase was uttered.

14. B: 'Engage the enemy more closely.'

The more famous signal, A, 'England expects that every man will do his duty', was sent at 11.45 a.m., but signal B was sent half an hour later, as battle was about to commence.

15. D: 'By The Sleepy Lagoon'

First recorded by Eric Coates with the Symphony Orchestra on 29 January 1942, you can still hear it every week on the BBC.

16. D: Tenth least corrupt

The UK is equal with Luxembourg and Germany. Denmark is the least corrupt country in the world, and North Korea, South Sudan and Somalia are rated the most corrupt nations, according to the Corruption Perceptions Index, an annual audit organized by international NGO Transparency International.

17. C: Three years

The proper length for a Victorian widow to mourn her husband was three years, the first year and a day of which was 'first mourning', when specific black mourning weeds were worn. But Queen Victoria set the example of mourning Prince Albert for 40 years. And by contrast, when a wife died, her husband was only expected to stay in mourning for three months.

18. A: Princess Anne

In 2002, appearing as Anne Elizabeth Alice Laurence v. Regina (i.e. v. her mum, the Queen) at Slough County Court, the Princess Royal was found guilty under the Dangerous Dogs Act after her English bull terrier Dotty bit two children in Windsor Great Park. She is the only senior royal ever to hold a criminal conviction. The Queen's personal dog psychologist Roger Mugford pleaded for Dotty's life to be spared, calling her an 'utterly placid, playful dog'.

19. B: Because you could buy one for £100

Lloyd George put them up for sale for £100 each, awarding 25,000 OBEs in five years. And the corrupt sale didn't end there. P. G. Wodehouse joked in one of his novels about peerages 'costing the deuce of a sum. Even baronetcies have gone up frightfully these days, I've been told.'

20. C: Classical marble sculptures taken from Greece by the Earl of Elgin to decorate his house in Scotland

At first, the Earl of Elgin only intended to make copies of the Greek antiquities. But he then removed the originals from the Parthenon and shipped them home for his private use. When his wife refused him conjugal relations, he was forced to sell them to the British Museum to fund his divorce. They have been a source of dispute between Britain and Greece ever since.

21. D: A disused air-raid shelter on Clapham Common

West Indians were actively recruited by the government to make up labour shortages after the end of the Second World War. Brixton was the nearest labour exchange to Clapham Common, so it became the first centre for the new West Indian settlers. But one arrival, John Richards, noted: 'They tell you it is the "mother country", you're all welcome, you all British. When you come here you realize you're a foreigner and that's all there is to it. The average person knows you as a colonial and that's all. You cut cane or carry bananas and that's it. Anybody wants to diddle you they say I just come off the banana boat and things like that.'

22. C: He resigned

Diamond was forced to resign following the Barclays Libor rate-rigging scandal in 2008 but wasn't subsequently sent to jail, unlike four Barclays traders.

23. D: Steve Morgan

In 2017, Steve Morgan, owner of house builder Redrow PLC, put £207 million of his company's shares into his own charity, the Morgan Foundation, which assists community groups and disabled children in the north-east.

24. C: 'You and I will be dead in three months' time.'

Churchill made the bleak prediction after Ismay had forecast that the British would win the Battle of Britain. Afterwards, Ismay said: 'I would prefer that this intimate heart to heart were never given to the world,' but it was included in David Reynolds' *In Command of History* published in 2005.

Section 2: Test 9

1. C: Cohabiting (but unmarried) couple

Unmarried cohabiting couple families have doubled in the period 1996–2016, while single-parent families grew by 18.6 per cent. Married couple households hardly changed, according to the Office of National Statistics.

2. C: A war between Scotland and England

After Henry VIII split England from Rome, he decided to attack Scotland in an attempt to weaken its ties with France. Together he considered them an invasion threat. His ultimate goal was to force marriage between Scottish King James V's daughter Mary and his own son Edward, thus forming a new alliance. 'We liked not the manner of the wooing,' a Scottish noble noted at the time, giving rise to the term. Too right, surely a box of Milk Tray would've done it?

3. FALSE

Captain Sarah West was the first Royal Navy Commander of a warship. She took command of HMS *Portland* in 2012 but resigned in 2014 over an alleged affair with a fellow officer.

4. D: The blood of Jesus

According to legend, Joseph of Arimathea visited Glastonbury in Somerset after Jesus' crucifixion and placed a chalice containing drops of his blood inside the well. Much folklore about Jesus himself visiting Cornwall and other parts of the south-west exists. William Blake's poem 'And did those feet in ancient time' (later set to music as a hymn and titled 'Jerusalem') is a famous example.

5. A: Cod

There had been several disputes over territorial fishing rights between the two countries, dating from the nineteenth century. However, in 1975 Iceland declared a 200-mile exclusive fishing zone, leading to the third Cod War, and threatened to leave NATO if challenged. Iceland got its way, and cod and chips became a lot more expensive for us Brits.

6. FALSE

In fact, 2,436 British bankers earned bonuses of over 1 million euros, while only 170 German bankers managed it.

7. C: The Chinese Restaurant, 1907

Situated in Glasshouse Street near London's Piccadilly Circus, the name was self-explanatory. It served chop suey (a Western invention) and sweet and sour pork, which shows that Londoners' tastes haven't really changed.

8. C: She wrote a play about him

When Pinter told his former lover he had written a play about their eight-year affair, she was 'deeply shocked' and set about writing a riposte. However, Bakewell waited until nine years after his death before allowing *Keeping in Touch* to be performed (on radio) in 2017. 'Harold would not be very pleased,' she admitted.

9. C: Too much sex

Victorians believed that human energy was finite and that expending it on frivolity reduced the chances of greatness. Excess ejaculation was known as spermatorrhea. Chastity and avoidance of masturbation were prescribed as treatments.

10. D: 'A drop in the bucket'

This is from the Bible (Isaiah 40:15).

11. B: Ben Kingsley

The son of a Yorkshire doctor, he won Best Actor for Richard Attenborough's *Gandhi* (1982). It won eight Oscars in all.

12. D: Reinforced steel

The door was made of Georgian oak until the 1991 IRA mortar attack, when it was replaced with bomb-proof steel. It takes eight men to lift it.

13. A and B: Groupthink and Doublespeak

'Groupthink' was coined by the journalist William Whyte after the publication of *1984*. 'Doublespeak' does not appear in the book either, although it may well have been created by combining the book's 'doublethink' and 'newspeak'. A forerunner of fake news? 'Miniluv' did appear in the book, as an abbreviation of the book's Ministry of Love (where torture took place), and 'Prolefeed' was Orwell's word for mindless entertainment for the masses.

14. A: 'As free and happy as Switzerland is today'

It is ironic that this idea first came from Churchill. Of course, Switzerland stayed neutral throughout the war and has never joined the European Union.

15. C: 300 years old

The coins must be over 300 years old and must also contain at least 10 per cent gold or silver. Alternatively, they may contain less silver and gold but be part of a hoard of ten or more. There are other such rules, governing objects made from prehistoric base metals and pottery, enforced by the Treasure Valuation Committee and Portable Antiquities Scheme.

16. D: Flatulence in the street

Challenging someone to fight, eavesdropping and being a common scold were all forbidden until 1967. But farting in the street has never been a criminal offence, funnily enough.

17. B: To avoid a mass grave for plague victims

These medieval plague pits, as they are known, exist all over London. When they were tunnelling for the Piccadilly Line where Brompton Road and Knightsbridge meet, they encountered a pit so dense with human remains that they had to dig round it.

18. C: Zealandia

She is the female personification of New Zealand and appeared on postage stamps in the early twentieth century. But 'Rule, Zealandia!' doesn't have quite the same ring to it, does it?

19. D: Louis Baboon

John Bull was a creation of eighteenth-century Scottish satirist Dr John Arbuthnot and first appeared in his scathing satire of the War of Spanish Succession called *Law Is a Bottomless Pit* (1712). In the satire, Bull (representing England) is suing Louis Baboon, a play on 'Bourbon', referring to Louis XIV of France.

20. B: Three nights in the stocks

Although D, a whipping, was added in 1530 by Henry VIII. A second offence could lead to an ear being cut off. A third offence meant the death penalty.

21. TRUE

When Soham murderer Ian Huntley was sent to prison in 2003, his former girlfriend Maxine Carr was given a new identity and leave to conceal her true background even from her child when it was born.

22. C: A pure finder

A pure finder sold dog faeces to the leather tanneries, where it was rubbed into the hides. Thus the nineteenth-century pavements had their own pooper-scoopers and were cleaner than they are today.

A tosher scavenged in the sewers, a chaunter sold sheet music and/or sang ballads for money, and a mudlark scavenged in river mud for valuables. Nowadays they'd all be rooting around for tat on eBay.

23. D: Martin Luther King Jr

Dr King came to London and gave the sermon on 6 December 1964 in front of 3,000 people. He was assassinated four years later.

24. B: 5 per cent

But in a recent Ipsos MORI poll, most of the British people questioned guessed the proportion of Muslims living in this country to be four times as high.

Section 2: Test 10

1. C: The area will become suitable for citrus cultivation

However, the same Met Office report suggests that sea levels could also rise by 40 cm in coastal areas like Newlyn in Cornwall, which, presumably, would make the area suitable for sole, rather than lemons.

2. D: Pollution was declared to be killing thousands

Committee chair Conservative MP Neil Parish said: 'Poor air quality is damaging the UK's environment and harming the nation's health: emissions have declined significantly over many decades, but not far enough to prevent the early deaths of 40–50,000 people each year.'

3. D: The UK

It has an average 694 people per square mile. Pakistan has 637, Nigeria has 539 and China has 372. But Bangladesh has 2,928 people per square mile, Taiwan has 1,683, and the Netherlands 1,069. In comparison, the UK still has plenty of room for population growth.

4. B: The Dambusters raid on Germany in 1943

British engineer Barnes Wallis perfected the idea of the 'bouncing bomb' after practising skimming marbles across a tub of water in his back garden. The drum-shaped bomb had to be dropped at a height of 60 feet by a Lancaster travelling at 232mph towards heavily defended German dams. Two out of three dams were breached in the Ruhr Valley, and 1,300 Germans were killed in the flooding which resulted.

5. A: The 1937 coronation of George VI

As the total number of TV sets manufactured by then was less than 20,000, this pioneering broadcast was only seen by the lucky few.

6. C: London theatre slang

In the 1950s and '60s theatre slang incorporated gay and Romany words and developed into a language called Polari. Other words now in the mainstream include 'slap' (make up) and 'ogle' (admire).

7. C: A dire warning

During a three-hour discussion regarding Diana's belongings and legacy in 2002, the Queen reportedly warned Burrell to be careful, adding: 'There are powers at work in this country about which we have no knowledge.' Burrell was subsequently charged with stealing from the estate of the Princess but acquitted after the intervention of Her Maj.

8. B: 'A bloody war or a sickly season'

In the nineteenth century, a bloody war or an epidemic causing many deaths among the ranks presented opportunities for quick promotion. 'A willing foe and sea room' is the toast on Friday.

9. FALSE

But it does misquote his famous signal from Trafalgar. It says: 'England expects every man to do his duty', whereas the words of the signal were actually: 'England expects that every man will do his duty'.

10. C: A Hyundai Santa Fe

Shackleton's great-grandson Patrick Bergel was the first to cross the Antarctic in a passenger car. His longest maintenance stop was 45 minutes to tighten a bolt.

11. B: It was the subject of the last successful blasphemy trial

The poem is written from the point of view of a Roman centurion who describes having sex with Jesus after his crucifixion, while also asserting that Jesus slept with his disciples, not to mention Roman emperor Pontius Pilate. Moral campaigner Mary Whitehouse sued the *Gay Times* where the poem first appeared and won. Blasphemy as a legal offence was abolished in 2008.

12. B: Britain and France uniting as one country

A formal Anglo-French union was considered by Churchill in 1940 as a way of avoiding French surrender to Germany. The British government approved of the declaration: 'France and Great Britain shall no longer be two nations, but one Franco-British Union'. However, France's Marshal Pétain rejected the idea, dismissively calling it 'fusion with a corpse'.

13. All of them

Some decline out of modesty, because they feel they don't deserve one; others decline in protest at some action of the government. In a letter to the Queen, John Lennon explained that he objected to Britain's involvement in the Nigerian civil war, British support for the Vietnam War, and 'Cold Turkey slipping down the charts'.

14. C: Pineapples symbolized peace, prosperity and status

They were introduced by Christopher Columbus and soon became a symbol of wealth and hospitality, as rich citizens were prepared to pay the equivalent of up to £5,000 for one to show off on their dining tables.

15. D: A sting jet

This is a concentrated area of high-velocity wind which sometimes arises at the tail end of a cloud formation when it clings to a low-pressure area. The phenomenon was unknown before the 1987 storm.

16. D: Drug dealing, prostitution, fraud, human trafficking and tax avoidance

The Bank report stated: 'The evidence available indicates that no more than half of Bank of England notes in circulation are likely to be held for use within the domestic economy for legitimate purposes.' The UK shadow or 'black' economy accounts for 10 per cent of UK GDP.

17. C: Dame Moura Lympany

All of pianist Moura Lympany's eight choices were from her own recordings. Soprano Elizabeth Schwarzkopf chose seven of her own out of the eight, comedian singer/songwriter Norman Wisdom chose five, and Rolf Harris three. Most Brits would regard this as rather a bit of a faux pas: as Shakespeare put it: 'We wound our modesty and make foul the clearness of our deservings, when of ourselves we publish them'.

18. C: Traces of cocaine

The survey was carried out by Real Radio Northwest journalists on baby-changing facilities in courts, churches, hospitals, police stations, supermarkets and pubs.

19. B: He sold fruit and vegetables

The term derives from a medieval apple known as a 'costard'.

20. B, C and D: Japanese Tosa, Dogo Argentino and Fila Brasiliero

Ownership can lead to a £5,000 fine and/or six months in prison. However, the 'Staffie' is not banned and is the third most popular breed in the UK.

21. All of them

Huxley also foresaw a technology which 'penetrates the mind, filling it with a babel of distractions . . . news items, mutually irrelevant bits of information, blasts of corybantic or sentimental music, continually repeated doses of drama that bring no catharsis, but merely create a craving for daily or even hourly emotional enemies'. In other words – the internet.

22. D: Fifth

According to the International Institute for Strategic Studies, the UK ranks fifth, behind, in order of spending, the US, China, Saudi Arabia and Russia.

23. D: Well-spoken people with a British accent

Mirren complained that Hollywood cast well-spoken British actors as baddies or 'snooty, stuck-up, malevolent creatures'.

24. A: 27.5 per cent

The top-earning 1 per cent (300,000 people) pay 27.5 per cent of all income tax. In spite of all that clever tax avoidance and offshore holdings.

1. TRUE

She is Baroness Smith of Basildon, Shadow Leader in the House of Lords.

2. C: The end of any royal reign by death or abdication

'Demise' is the legal term for the end of a reign. The Demise of the Crown Act, going back to 1702, ensures that on death or abdication the title passes smoothly to the succeeding monarch. The king is dead: long live the king (or queen). No need for a battle in a muddy field.

3. C: Frigg was the goddess of love

(Although she does also give her name to Friday, 'the day of Frigg'). The chief Anglo-Saxon god was Woden. Rather charmingly the god of the sea was Wade.

4. B and C: New Zealand and Great Britain

However, when the England team faces another of Britain's nations on the football pitch, to avoid confusion 'God Save The Queen' is usually replaced with 'Land Of Hope And Glory' or 'I Vow To Thee My Country'. The Scots play 'Flower Of Scotland', and the Welsh sing 'Land of My Fathers'. But the Northern Irish team sticks with 'God Save The Queen'.

5. A: Grounds for divorce

And it is still considered adultery even if you are separated from your husband or wife.

6. A and B: An interview without coffee, and a carpet parade

Both refer to Army disciplinary meetings. C is the equivalent in the RAF.

7. B: To jump the queue in the London Underground ticket hall

The last time anyone was arrested under this old bye-law is unknown.

8. C: 'The Star Spangled Banner'

John Stafford Smith was a British composer, and the original version was the song of the Anacreontic Society, a gentleman's club in London. The patriotic American lyrics were added later during the American War of Independence, and it was adopted as the American national anthem in 1931.

9. D: 13 per cent

13 per cent of the UK's population is foreign born, according to the last Census. But in an Ipsos MORI poll, most people canvassed thought the proportion was closer to 25 per cent, almost twice as high as the reality.

10. TRUE

General Brooke intended to use mustard gas on the beaches if the Germans invaded Britain. Churchill also advocated its use '100 per cent'. He said: 'It is absurd to consider morality on this topic when everyone used it in the last war without a word of complaint.'

11. C: The monarch's panel of advisers drawn from senior politicians and civil servants, as well as other royals

The Privy Council has roughly 600 members, but a full meeting is only required on the engagement, abdication or death of the monarch. Membership comes with the right to call yourself 'the Right Honourable'. Initiation into the council requires new members to kneel on a stool before the monarch and kiss his/her hand. Labour MP and republican Tony Benn refused to comply. 'I always put my thumb out and kissed my thumb,' he noted in his diaries.

12. C: He inspired Tony Blair to form New Labour

Tony Blair mentioned Mondeo Man at the 1996 Labour Party conference after meeting the owner of a Ford Mondeo (then a popular mass-market saloon) while out canvassing. The Mondeo driver was an ex Labour voter who'd bought his own council house, not to mention his car, and was happily self-employed. He told the Labour leader he intended to vote Tory at the next election. Blair told the conference: 'He crystallized for me the basis of our [Labour's] failure . . . His instincts were to get on in life. And he thought our instincts were to stop him. But that was never our history or our purpose.'

13. C: Stonehenge

King Arthur's wizard Merlin, visiting aliens and the Romans have all at various times been cited as the builders of the famous stone monument in Wiltshire. However, it is now generally accepted that it was constructed by local tribes. The largest 25-ton sarsen stones come from Marlborough Downs 20 miles away. The smaller four-ton 'bluestones' were quarried from the Preseli mountains in south-west Wales. How they were transported 240 miles by Neolithic people in 2500 BC remains a matter for conjecture.

14. A: A gay hang-out

A 'molly' was a slang word for a gay man, and molly houses were inns, taverns or coffeehouses where homosexuals met. One such establishment was Mother Clap's Molly House, on Field Lane in Holborn.

15. FALSE

It's even higher than that. The UK is £1.73 trillion in debt, according to the Office of National Statistics, December 2016. However, the UK earns over £2 trillion each year, so if we just survived a year on rations of bread and dripping we'd be sorted.

16. All of them

John Lennon was the subject of protracted harassment from US
authorities regarding his right to permanent residence. Under orders
from President Nixon, the FBI compiled a 3,000-page file on
Lennon as a result of his anti-Vietnam War activism and made
several attempts to deport him. Sid Vicious was arrested for murder
in New York; Ozzy Osbourne was arrested for urinating on the
Alamo Cenotaph while wearing a dress; and Liam Gallagher was
gently reprimanded for dribbling beer at the MTV Awards.

17. C: To make it support a war

Prime Minister Anthony Eden had launched a highly controversial
invasion of Egypt (with France and Israel) intending to assassinate
President Nasser and gain control of the Suez Canal. The BBC
came under pressure from the government to support its
propaganda for the war, and when it refused, Eden, according to his
press secretary William Clarke, planned to 'take over the BBC
altogether and subject it wholly to the will of the government'.
According to Dr Alban Webb, author of *London Calling: Britain,
the BBC World Service and the Cold War*: 'It ranks as the most
serious argument between the BBC and the government of
all time.'

18. TRUE

In 1983, engineering firm LinktoEurope dismissed a tunnel as
'impractical' and submitted plans to the government for a
21-mile suspension bridge starting at Folkestone or Dover. It
was to be suspended on 15 giant piers and hang 220 feet above
the Channel, with an estimated cost of £3 billion. According to
the National Archives, the Channel Tunnel, which was built
instead, ended up costing £4.65 billion, almost double the original
estimate.

19. C: Wiltshire

An underground complex in Corsham, Wiltshire, was designated as the Emergency Government War Headquarters in the late 1950s. The kilometre-long bunker could support 4,000 government ministers and civil servants. It had its own bakery and medical centre, but the only special privilege afforded the prime minister's bedroom was that, instead of bare concrete, it was painted white. Poignantly, the bunker also contained a library of maps, scientific and technical documents as well as Acts of Parliament so that Britain could be rebuilt. A skeleton staff kept the bunker operational until the mid 1990s.

20. C: They have all caused a royal scandal

They have all fallen foul of royal etiquette regarding touching members of the Royal Family. In 2014, James put his arm round the Duchess of Cambridge while presenting her with a souvenir shirt. In 2009, Michelle Obama hugged the Queen, and in 1992, while Australian prime minister, Keating put his arm round Her Majesty, earning himself the nickname the 'Lizard of Oz'. In 2015, Australian businesswoman Janine Kirk struck back for the ladies by placing a hand on Prince Charles's buttocks (a claim she denied). Official Palace advice states: 'There are no obligatory codes of behaviour when meeting The Queen or a member of the Royal Family, but many people wish to observe the traditional forms.'

21. FALSE

South Korea does, followed by Ireland and Hong Kong. UK is 23rd in the league table in internet speeds and has some catching up to do to stay in the global game.

22. A: Italy

Italy has 51 Cultural World Heritage Sites, China has 48, France has 41 and the UK has 29. However, UNESCO's criteria for awarding the prized status are questionable. In 2015, it certified a Fray Bentos meat-packing plant in Uruguay as a World Heritage Site. The committee felt the factory deserved equal status with places such as India's Taj Mahal because it 'illustrates the whole process of meat sourcing, processing, packing and dispatching'. Mind you, eight of Britain's World Heritage Sites are equally focused on the country's social and industrial, rather than artistic and architectural, heritage (e.g. Blaenavon Industrial Landscape, and Saltaire village in West Yorkshire).

23. A: Tony Blair

Worryingly for Blair, the Iraq War hadn't even started then either. Katie Price, aka Jordan, came second and Mrs Thatcher third. A separate BBC History poll on the same subject nominated Jack the Ripper. If the poll were rerun today, which personality might topple Blair from his winner's pedestal?

24. C: A Teletubby

O2 contractors accidentally dug up a time capsule buried by BBC children's TV programme *Blue Peter* in 1998 containing, amongst other things, a Teletubby and a Blue Peter badge. Surely we achieved more than that in the 1990s?

25. C: The dog's bollocks

A, 'the cat's pyjamas', and B, 'the bee's knees', are American in origin, examples from a spate of animal/body-part slang denoting excellence which became popular in 1920s. 'The ant's pants', 'the tiger's spots' and, less pithily, 'the elephant's adenoids' were also available. Perhaps unsurprisingly the Brits came up with the earthier 'dog's bollocks', a coinage recorded in Eric Partridge's 1949 *Dictionary of Slang and Unconventional English*. By contrast, the 1937 edition of the same book records D, 'the dog's breakfast', as denoting 'a mess'.

The publishers wish to thank all those whose words embellish this quiz book. Many of the quotes were found in anthologies and on internet sites. With apologies to those authors whose words we were unable to source, the quotes in the book include the following:

p.2: John Mortimer, *Famous Trials*; **p.5:** Boris Johnson, *Telegraph;* **p.8:** Caitlin Moran, *The Times*; **p.11:** Kathy Lette, *Altar Ego*; **p.17:** Spike Milligan, *Rommel? Gunner Who?* **p.18:** Jeremy Lloyd, *Are You Being Served?;* **p.19:** Johnny Speight, *Till Death Us Do Part;* **p. 30:** James Bond – *You Only Live Twice* screenplay by Roald Dahl; **p.33:** Tom Stoppard, *Jumpers*; **p.35:** Dawn French and Jennifer Saunders, *French & Saunders Live*; **p.40:** George Orwell, *Why I Write*; **p.48:** John Cleese and Connie Booth, *Fawlty Towers*; **p.51:** Clive James, *Telegraph*; **p.53:** Pete Doherty, *Metro*; **p.56:** Matt Groening, *The Simpsons*; **p.57:** Joss Whedon, *Buffy the Vampire Slayer*; **p.62:** Caitlin Moran, *Moranthology*; **p.64:** C. S. Lewis, *God in the Dock*; **p.76:** Neil Wilson & 7 more, *Lonely Planet Guide to Britain*; **p.82:** Julian Barnes, *Talking It Over*; **p.84:** William Golding, *Fire Down Below*; **p.88:** Paul Theroux, *The Kingdom by the Sea*; **p.91:** Richard Curtis, *Love, Actually*; **p.100:** Antony Jay and Jonathan Lynn, *Yes, Prime Minister*; **pp.107, 123:** George Mikes, *How to be an Alien*; **p.117:** Alan Ayckbourn, from Gyles Brandreth interview, *Telegraph*; **p.119:** P. G. Wodehouse, *Mr Mulliner Speaking*; **p.121:** Bertrand Russell, *Marriage and Morals*; **p.126:** Christopher Hitchens, *Hitch-22, A Memoir*; **p.129:** Hugh Dennis, *Mock the Week*; **p.134:** Jimmy Perry and David Croft, *Dad's Army*; **p.138:** Alexander McCall Smith, *Friends, Lovers, Chocolate*; **p.144:** Bernard Levin, *The Times*; **p.149:** P. J. O'Rourke, *National Lampoon*; **p.152:** John O'Farrell, *An Utterly Impartial History of Britain*; **p.161:** Evelyn Waugh, *The Loved One*; **pp.162, 169:** Antony Jay and Jonathan Lynn, *Yes, Minister*; **p.165:** Mark Haddon interviewed by Horatia Harrod in the *Telegraph*; **p.167:** John

Cleese and Charles Crighton, *A Fish Called Wanda*; **p.171:** Martin Amis interviewed by Alexandra Topping, *Guardian*; **p.180:** Matt Lucas and David Walliams, *Little Britain*; **p.183:** George Orwell, *England, Your England*; **pp.195, 203, 217, 227, 254:** W. C. Sellar and R. J. Yeatman, *1066 and All That*

Acknowledgements

I would like to thank Marianne Velmans, whose idea this book was. When the editor of a Britishness quiz book turns out to be Dutch, the author half-Bolivian and the copy editor Ailsa Bathgate Scottish, I think that says something about our country.

With their expert smelting of facts and crafting of nuance, this book has evolved from Neolithic dustbin lid into the solid, query-proof inlaid Bronze Age shield you now hold in your hands.

I would like to acknowledge the help of John Lewis-Stempel, whose work proved an invaluable source. Likewise Chris Bryant MP for his books on parliament and the Office for National Statistics, who are just amazing.

There have been innumerable other sources and I'd like to thank them as well as Boudicca, Glenn Hoddle, Charles I and Pulp for making the journey through British culture and history so interesting.

Which of the following truly originated in Britain?

A: St George

B: Teabags

C: Pubs

D: Fish and chips

What qualifications does the Queen have?

Are you Britain's biggest plonker or the dog's bollocks?

Which Briton was the first to circumnavigate the world?

What is Jodrell Bank?

Who are 'les goddams'?

What was the 1986 Salmon Act?